COUNTRIES OF THE WORLD

Taiwan

Gareth Stevens Publishing
A WORLD ALMANAC EDUCATION GROUP COMPANY

About the Author: Michaela Ryan is a writer based in Melbourne, Australia. She has honors degrees in Law and Arts from Monash University. She studied at Tokyo University in 1996 and 1997 and became fascinated with Asian culture. She has since written legal, financial, and travel articles for many magazines — both in print and online. She last visited Taiwan in December 2002, when she interviewed government officials and business leaders for a business magazine.

PICTURE CREDITS

Agence France Presse: 78, 79, 80, 81 (both), 85 (both)
Art Directors/TRIP Photo Library: 3 (bottom), 5, 6, 7, 8, 9 (top), 18, 27, 32, 34, 35 (top), 38 (top), 39, 47, 50, 51, 55, 56, 59, 60, 61, 62, 63, 64, 66, 67, 70 (both), 72, 73, 91
Bes Stock Photo Library: cover, 1, 24, 31, 42, 44 (bottom)
Michelle Burgess: 9 (bottom), 48
Focus Team Photo Agency & Press: 4, 22, 52, 71, 87
Getty Images/Hulton Archive: 10, 12, 14, 15 (top), 37, 49, 53, 74, 76, 77
The Hutchison Library: 2, 3 (top and center), 16, 17, 21 (top), 25, 29, 33, 40, 44 (top), 57, 69, 89
Lonely Planet Images: 38 (bottom), 45, 58, 84
Melvin Neo: 75
North Wind Picture Archives: 11
David Simson: 13, 19, 20, 21 (bottom), 23, 26 (top), 28 (both), 30, 35 (bottom), 36, 41 (both), 43, 46, 54, 65, 68
Taiwan Visitors Center: 15 (bottom)
Topham Picturepoint: 82, 83
Travel Ink Photo and Feature Library: 26 (bottom)

Digital Scanning by Superskill Graphics Pte Ltd

Written by
MICHAELA RYAN

Edited by
MELVIN NEO

Edited in the U.S. by
ALAN WACHTEL
CATHERINE GARDNER

Designed by
LYNN CHIN

Picture research by
SUSAN JANE MANUEL

First published in North America in 2003 by
Gareth Stevens Publishing
A World Almanac Education Group Company
330 West Olive Street, Suite 100
Milwaukee, Wisconsin 53212 USA

Please visit our web site at
www.garethstevens.com
For a free color catalog describing
Gareth Stevens Publishing's list of high-quality
books and multimedia programs, call
1-800-542-2595 (USA) or 1-800-387-3178 (Canada).
Gareth Stevens Publishing's fax: (414) 332-3567.

Originated and designed by
Times Editions
An imprint of Times Media Private Limited
A member of the Times Publishing Group
Times Centre, 1 New Industrial Road
Singapore 536196
http://www.timesone.com.sg/te

Library of Congress Cataloging-in-Publication Data
Ryan, Michaela.
Taiwan/ by Michaela Ryan.
p. cm. — (Countries of the world)
Summary: Provides an overview of the geography, history, government, lifestyle, language, art, and food of Taiwan, exploring its customs and current issues.
Includes bibliographical references and index.
ISBN 0-8368-2368-0 (lib. bdg.)
1. Taiwan— Juvenile literature. [1. Taiwan.] I. Title.
II. Countries of the world.
(Milwaukee, Wis.)
DS799.R9 2003
951.24′9—dc21 2003042394

Printed in Singapore

1 2 3 4 5 6 7 8 9 07 06 05 04 03

Contents

AN OVERVIEW OF TAIWAN

Taiwan is a country full of beautiful mountains and unique wildlife. The tranquillity of the nation's countryside contrasts starkly to its bustling, chaotic major cities. Agriculture was once a huge industry in this country, but these days, Taiwan is known for its dazzling electronics and technology.

Some aboriginal people in Taiwan are trying to preserve their culture from the rapid changes taking place around them. A majority of Taiwanese are of Chinese descent, and hence, Taiwanese culture has largely been adapted from Chinese traditions. Although the official name of Taiwan is the "Republic of China," in this book, we simply refer to the country as Taiwan because this is its most commonly used name.

Opposite: **The changing of the guard ceremony takes place every hour at the Revolutionary Martyrs' Shrine in the city of Taipei.**

Below: **School children wave their flags as they celebrate Taiwan's Double Tenth National Day, on October 10.**

THE FLAG OF TAIWAN

The current national flag of Taiwan was adopted on December 17, 1928, after the unification of China. The Taiwanese flag is red with a blue rectangle at the top left corner. A white sun is positioned at the center of the blue rectangle. The twelve points of the sun represent the twelve periods of two hours that take place each day. Lu Hao-tung, the designer of the symbol, saw the points of the sun as symbolizing the continuous progress of the Chinese revolution. The colors blue, white, and red represent the Three Principles of the People of Taiwan: nationalism, democracy, and social well-being.

Geography

Shaped like a sweet potato, Taiwan has an area of 13,888 square miles (35,980 square kilometers). Taiwan is located among a chain of islands in eastern Asia that reach up to Japan in the north and down to the Philippines in the southwest. The country is made up of the main island, called Taiwan, and the Penghu Archipelago, which includes islands such as Lutao, Lanyu, and the Penghu Islands. The islands of Taiwan are surrounded by the East China Sea, Pacific Ocean, Philippine Sea, South China Sea, and Taiwan Strait. Taiwan also claims some other islands including the Chinmen Islands, which are also claimed by mainland China, and the Spratly Islands, which are located far to the south and are also claimed by China, Brunei, Malaysia, the Philippines, and Vietnam.

THE PENGHU ISLANDS

Also known as the Pescadores, this group of islands boasts natural harbors and abundant marine life. Many of the islands' residents are fishermen who lead simple lives.

(A Closer Look, page 60)

Left: **The volcanic beach on Lutao, or Green Island, includes a number of hot springs. Green Island is located off the east coast of Taiwan, about 20.5 miles (33 km) from the city of Taitung.**

Left: **Yu Shan is the country's highest point. Taiwan was once covered in trees. Although the country's mountains still boast lush green forests, only 55 percent of the land is covered with trees.**

Mountains and Plains

On the main island of Taiwan, a range of mountains called the Chungyang Shanmo (CHONG-yuhng SHUHN-mor) covers half the land. Prehistoric volcanoes rose from the sea and formed the range that extends from the island's northeast to its south. Along the tops of the mountain ranges, inactive volcanoes continue to provide hot mineral springs.

The highest point of the Chungyang Shanmo is Yu Shan (Mount Jade) at 13,113 feet (3,997 m) high. Yu Shan also houses a wildlife reserve. From December to May, the peak of Mount Jade is covered in snow.

To the east of the Chungyang Shanmo, facing the Pacific Ocean, the mountains form steep cliffs that are 2,500 feet (760 m) high. West of the mountains are foothills, as well as flat, fertile plains and basins that slope smoothly toward the Taiwan Strait.

Rivers

The island has more than one hundred rivers and streams. In the west, deposits of sediments from rivers have filled in the shallow coastal waters. As a result, the land has been extended. This has given Taiwan additional land that is useful both for its natural resources and for agriculture.

Climate

The southern part of Taiwan enjoys a tropical climate and warm oceans. In contrast, the north of the country has a subtropical climate in the mountain areas and even experiences some snow.

The main island experiences heavy rainfall throughout the year. In the south, the southwest monsoon begins in May or June and lasts until August or September. Thundershowers and strong tropical storms known as typhoons bring abundant rainfall. Northern Taiwan remains relatively dry during this period. The northeast monsoon, however, brings heavy rainfall to the northern regions from October to March. These rains combine for approximately 99 inches (2,515 millimeters) of rainfall per year.

Summer, from May to September, is hot and humid with an average temperature of 86° Fahrenheit (30° Celsius). Winter, from December to February, is short and mild with temperatures around 59° F (15° C). The temperature rarely drops below 41° F (5° C).

Spring, in April and May, and fall, in October and November, provide the most pleasant climate as there is limited rainfall. The weather during the day is fine, and the nights are slightly cool.

***Above:* In the mountainous area north of the tropic of Cancer that runs through Taiwan, the climate is subtropical, and it is common to see snow in the higher elevations of mountains such as Hohuan Shan.**

TYPHOONS

Typhoons are tropical cyclones with strong winds and heavy rainfall. When a typhoon hits, it can do a lot of damage. Often, a typhoon will uproot trees, demolish entire buildings, and cause severe floods.
(A Closer Look, page 72)

Plants and Animals

Taiwan's diverse climate and landscape allow a wide range of flora and fauna to thrive on the island. Estimates indicate that there are 17,600 species of insects, including 400 species of butterflies, about 60 types of mammals, nearly 500 kinds of different birds, 90 types of reptiles, 30 types of amphibians, and 150 species of freshwater fish in and around Taiwan. Common animals in the country include monkeys, deer, wild boars, goats, pheasants, and geese.

One exotic animal found in Tawian is the Formosan macaque, a type of monkey with origins in mainland Asia. These monkeys live in low-lying mountains in the northeast and southwest of Taiwan as well as areas close to the sea.

Over 4,000 species of vascular plants are found in Taiwan. In the highest peaks, coniferous forests exist. Rhododendrons, junipers, and Japanese cedars are plentiful in the hills and mountains. In the lower areas, palms and bamboo can be found. Illegal loggers, or people who illegally chop down trees for their wood, are severely punished. The government plans for reforestation, even though over half of Taiwan is covered with trees. Some of the trees in Taiwan are over one hundred years old.

THE POINSETTIA

Although the poinsettia originated in Mexico, this beautiful flower also thrives in parts of Taiwan that have a similar climate. The scenic Sun Moon Lake (*above*) is one such area.

Left: **The muntjac, a small barking deer, is one of Taiwan's rarest species. About 60 percent of the wild animal species found in Taiwan are unique and cannot be found anywhere else in the world. Taiwan has such a high proportion of endemic species because of its geographical isolation.**

History

People of Malayan-Polynesian backgrounds were probably the earliest inhabitants of Taiwan. The culture of these aboriginal people was similar to the culture of the people of Indonesia. As people from the Chinese mainland arrived, they pushed the aborigines into the mountains. The island also came to serve as a base for Chinese and Japanese pirates, who found Taiwan's location ideal for attacks on trade routes.

In the sixteenth century, the first westerners reached Taiwan. The Dutch came to live on the island in the early 1620s. A Dutch fortress was established on a southwestern peninsula known then as Tayouan, meaning "terrace bay." Sugar and rice were grown during this period, and churches and forts were built.

The Dutch employed the Chinese people already living in Taiwan. They also brought over Chinese laborers from China. Although some of these laborers returned to China, others remained on the island and married local aborigines. These people are the ancestors of today's Taiwanese population.

EARLY EUROPEAN CONTACT

The Dutch explorer, Jan Huyghen van Linschoten (1563-1611) (*left*), who served as navigator on a Portuguese ship in the late sixteenth century, was among the first westerners to visit Taiwan. Van Linschoten named the island *Ilha Formosa*, which means "beautiful island," and it was known as Formosa for the next four centuries.

(A Closer Look, page 50)

The Chinese Take Over

Above: **This hand-painted woodcut print depicts Chinese pirate ships attacking a trade ship. Located along the main sea routes, Taiwan was an ideal base for pirates.**

Dutch rule ended in 1661, when the Chinese pirate Cheng Cheng-kung took over the island. Cheng, who was also known as Koxinga, came to the island to escape the rule of the new Ching (Qing) dynasty in China and make a base for his army. Cheng held siege over the Dutch for two years before successfully claiming Taiwan. Cheng's son, Cheng Ching, succeeded him.

Ching dynasty troops from China, also known as Manchus, arrived in Taiwan in 1683 and defeated Cheng's son. China then claimed that Taiwan was a prefecture of the Fukien province of China. There was, however, not much evidence of Taiwan being of any importance to China at this time.

During the seventeenth century, people from mainland China, many of whom were trying to escape wars and food shortages, flocked to Taiwan. Soon, the island's population had increased tenfold. The majority of ethnic Chinese living in Taiwan today are descendants of Chinese immigrants who arrived during this time.

In 1886, the Ching dynasty authorities of China declared that Taiwan was a province of the Chinese Empire. This was a response to Japan's increasing influence in Asia.

Japanese Rule

In 1895, the Manchus were defeated by the Japanese in the Sino-Japanese War. To end the war, China signed the Treaty of Shimonoseki, which surrendered Taiwan to Japan.

On May 25, 1895, the Taiwan Republic was founded by a group of leading Taiwanese with the assistance of Chinese officials. Four days later, the Japanese army arrived in northern Taiwan to fight this independence movement. The fight to reestablish Japanese rule ended on October 21, 1895, when the Japanese took over Tainan, the designated capital of the independent Taiwan Republic.

Japanese rule was harsh in the following years, and many uprisings occurred. During Japan's rule, however, schools, roads, transportation systems, agriculture, and industries were developed.

Taiwan During World War II

In 1943, the Allied Powers signed the Cairo Declaration. The declaration said that, once Japan was defeated, Taiwan would be returned to China, which was then under the rule of Chiang Kai-shek and the *Kuomintang* (KHUO-min-dunk). When the war

Above: **On December 26, 1939, General Chiang Kai-shek (1888-1975) arrived in Taipei for a meeting of the Kuomintang Nationalist Party congress. At the meeting, he was named president of the Executive Yuan.**

CHIANG KAI-SHEK

The leader of China's nationalist Kuomintang, Chiang Kai-shek was overthrown by the communist regime in 1949. He was forced to move to Taiwan where he ruled the country until his death in 1975.

(*A Closer Look, page 49*)

ended in 1945, Chiang Kai-shek's troops occupied Taiwan on behalf of the Allied forces. The Taiwanese were happy to see the end of Japanese rule. A new educational system was developed, and citizens were sent to the United States to learn new technologies.

In time, many Taiwanese saw the Chinese regime was corrupt and cruel. On February 28, 1947, the Taiwanese showed their anger, and demonstrations occurred in Taipei. The Kuomintang secretly sent troops to kill Taiwanese who it viewed as a threat to its rule. Between 18,000 and 28,000 people, among them doctors, lawyers, and students, fell victim to this plan.

In 1949, communists overthrew the Kuomintang in China. Chiang fled to Taiwan and continued to enforce strict martial law there. He restricted the people's freedom and controlled the country's politics, media, armed forces, and educational system.

The 1952 San Francisco Peace Treaty that ended World War II promised that Taiwan's status would be decided according to the United Nations charter. No formal decision, however, was ever made, and Chiang continued his dictatorial rule. Many countries considered Chiang's Kuomintang to be the true government not only of Taiwan, but also of mainland China, though it held no power over the mainland communist government.

***Below:* The walls of the Chiang Kai-shek Memorial Hall in the city of Taipei are covered with framed photographs that provide a record of the country's political history.**

Modern Times

Although the United Nations recognized the Kuomintang as the legitimate government of both mainland China and Taiwan after World War II, Taiwan—the last stronghold of the Kuomintang—was expelled from the United Nations in 1971. Its seat was given to the communist government of mainland China. Then in 1972, the United States and mainland China entered an agreement known as the Shanghai Communique that established the U.S. policy of recognizing "One China." Taiwan became seen as part of China, even though its government worked independently.

Chiang Kai-shek died in 1975. His son, Chiang Ching-kuo, served as president from 1978 until his death in 1988, when his vice president, Lee Teng-hui, took over. In March 1996, Lee won Taiwan's first direct presidential election. He lost in 2000 to Chen Shui-bian of the Democratic Progressive Party, ending a half-century of Kuomintang rule. The new president has pledged support for economic development and stability in relations with China.

Below: Taiwan's newly elected president, Chen Shui-bian (_left_), and vice president, Annette Lu (_right_), celebrate after Chen's victory in Taiwan's second presidential elections, held on March 18, 2000.

Cheng Cheng-kung (1624–62)

A Ming loyalist from China, Cheng Cheng-kung was also known as Koxinga. Establishing his base in Taiwan, he hoped to restore the Ming dynasty. Cheng was successful in forcing the Dutch out of Taiwan in 1661, and under his rule, the strong Chinese influence in Taiwan first appeared. He introduced Chinese laws and customs, built schools, and established Taiwan's first Confucian temple. During his rule, many Chinese immigrated to Taiwan.

Lee Teng-hui (1923–)

The first local-born president of Taiwan, Lee Teng-hui came to power in 1988. In 1996, he was reelected by popular vote, becoming the first democratically elected president of Taiwan. Although Lee was a member of the Kuomintang, whose previous administrations had seen themselves as the rulers of both Taiwan and mainland China, he supported the idea of an independent Taiwan. One of Lee's legacies as president was his promotion of ethnic unity. He tried to reduce the tension between immigrant Taiwanese and those who were born in Taiwan, introducing the idea of "New Taiwanese" to show that even new arrivals should be considered Taiwanese.

Lee Teng-hui

Annette Hsiu-lien Lu (1944–)

Lu graduated from National Taiwan University with a law degree. She then studied at the University of Illinois and Harvard University in the United States. In 1978, during a difficult time in Taiwan when many people were leaving the country, Lu left her studies and returned to Taiwan to run for election to the National Assembly. During her campaign, she spoke out against government abuses, and in 1979, Lu was sentenced to twelve years in prison for making a speech about human rights. After serving part of the sentence, she was allowed to leave for cancer treatment. In various official positions, Lu has promoted human rights, Taiwan's role in the United Nations, protection for the environment, and women's and children's safety. On March 18, 2000, she was elected vice president of Taiwan.

Annette Lu

Government and the Economy

Taiwan has held democratic national elections since 1996. Before then, the country was ruled under martial law enforced by the unelected Kuomintang party. Today, Taiwan's leader is its president, who is elected to a four-year term. The president is the commander of the armed services and has authority over each of the five branches of government, called *yuan* (YUEN). These are the Executive, Legislative, Control, Judicial, and Examination Yuan.

ADMINISTRATIVE REGIONS

Taiwan is divided into several administrative divisions, including sixteen counties, five municipalities, and two special municipalities.

Above: **The Taipei City Government Building is a modern structure that reflects the dynamic economy of the country.**

The Branches of Government

The president appoints the premier, who leads the Executive Yuan, the most powerful of all of the government's divisions. The premier and a group of officers make up a council that is responsible for policy and administrative matters.

The Legislative Yuan and the National Assembly are the lawmaking bodies. The Legislative Yuan is the highest lawmaking body in Taiwan. It currently has 225 members, who serve three-year terms. The 300-member National Assembly only convenes to consier constitutional amendments, presidential impeachment, or the alteration of national boundaries.

Taiwan has a multiparty democratic system of government. The two main parties in the National Assembly and Legislative Yuan are the Kuomintang and the Democratic Progressive Party. Before March 1989, when opposition parties were legalized, the Kuomintang ruled unchallenged. In the 2001 election, however, the New Party, the People First Party, and the Taiwan Solidarity Union all won seats. Taiwan today has almost 100 political parties.

The Control Yuan oversees public services. It tries to ensure efficiency and stamp out corruption. Its twenty-nine members are appointed by the president and approved by the Legislative Yuan. Members serve for six years before being replaced with new appointees. In recent times, this branch has been responsible for major investigations into corruption and the impeachment of those who are corrupt.

Below: The Presidential Building in Taipei used to house the office of the Taiwan Governor-General during the Japanese occupation of Taiwan. Construction of the building began on June 1, 1912, and was completed in March 1919.

The president also appoints the members of the Examination Yuan to six-year terms. This branch of government oversees Taiwan's civil service. It conducts civil service, professional, and technical examinations, and it is in chrage of the government's personnel system.

The Judicial Yuan is the head of the legal system. Taiwan follows the civil law system. Under the civil law system, disputes are settled according to a written legal code determined through a legislative process.

TAINAN

Taiwan's ancient capital, the city of Tainan, is located on the southwestern coast of the country's main island and boasts many landmarks of historical significance. It was chosen as the country's first capital by Cheng Cheng-kung in the seventeenth century.

(A Closer Look, page 66)

Rapidly Growing Economy

Taiwan has enjoyed several decades of rapid economic growth. The average economic growth rate from 1952 to 1999 was 8 percent. This rate of growth was much higher than that of almost every other country in the world during that time. Taiwan's exports increased rapidly, spurring the industrialization of the country. The country has done so well that it maintains a trade surplus and has among the world's largest foreign reserves.

Before the 1960s, agriculture was Taiwan's main industry, comprising about 35 percent of the economy. This was partly due to the fact that the government heavily subsidized the agricultural industry. These days, there is far more diversity within Taiwan's economy, and the contribution of agriculture dropped to just 2 percent in 2001. Nevertheless, one major crop that is still grown in Taiwan is rice. Fruits, sugarcane, vegetables, and tea are other crops also grown. In addition, there is some livestock farming in the country, with farmers rearing hogs, poultry, and dairy cows, and the fishing industry is large.

Above: **Chi-Lung (Keelung) was opened as a commercial port in 1863. Since then, Chi-Lung Harbor has made great progress and ranks as one of the world's largest seaports.**

With its agricultural industry in decline, Taiwan's economy has shifted focus to other industries. While the country depended on more labor-intensive industries in the past, these are being replaced by more capital- and technology-intensive industries, which provide much higher rates of profits. In recent times, Taiwan's major exports have been machinery, electronic products, clothing, and communications equipment. The country's exports go mainly to the United States (23.5 percent), Hong Kong (21.1 percent), and Europe (16 percent).

THE ELECTRONICS INDUSTRY

Taiwan is a leading manufacturer in the electronics industry, and it produces semiconductors, computers, and other information industry products for leading companies worldwide.
(A Closer Look, page 52)

A Technologically Advanced Society

In 2000, there were 16 million mobile phones users in Taiwan out of a population of 22 million. Taiwanese companies produced 34 million mobile phones in 2001 — 6 percent of the world's output. The country also boasts numerous Internet service providers and, by late 2001, there were 11.6 million active Internet users in Taiwan. Taiwan's telecommunications system is also considered to be among the best in Asia outside of Japan.

Below: **Most Taiwanese have mobile phones. They are a convenient way of keeping in touch with friends and family.**

People and Lifestyle

The Taiwanese are relatively wealthy, and many of them choose to travel overseas every year. Overseas travel is so popular that the government has introduced programs to encourage Taiwanese people to spend their holidays in Taiwan.

Some parents send their children of elementary school age to summer camps in the United States. A recent trend has been for both children and teenagers to attend camps in the United States, England, and Canada, where they can learn English.

Eighty-four percent of Taiwan's population are either Fujianese or Hakka. The Fujianese came from the Fujian Province in China, while the Hakka came from the Guangdong Province in China. Fourteen percent of Taiwanese people are Chinese immigrants who have arrived from mainland China since World War II. There used to be more tension between Taiwanese whose ancestors emigrated from China long ago and more recent immigrants, but former president Lee Teng-hui increased national unity by calling immigrants "New Taiwanese."

ABORIGINES AND HAKKAS

Descendants of the original inhabitants of Taiwan still live in the country today. Many of them have adopted modern clothing and habits, but some still observe traditional customs.

(A Closer Look, page 44)

Below: **Many Taiwanese keep abreast of current trends in music and fashion. Teenagers often sport the latest Western styles in clothing and accessories.**

Left: A woman in a park in the city of Taichung sings karaoke, one of the many pastimes enjoyed by older Taiwanese. Average life expectancy in Taiwan is about 75 years and, according to 1999 government statistics, about 8 percent of the population is over 65.

Only 2 percent of the population is made up of native aborigines. Taiwan is home to several different aboriginal groups, and each speaks its own tribal language. With the modernization of Taiwan, many aborigines have left their traditional roles as hunters or farmers and have taken jobs in factories. Aborigines generally have lower levels of education and wealth compared to other Taiwanese. The government has tried to improve this situation by introducing scholarships for aborigines to study in good schools.

Taiwan's population density was the second highest in the world in 2000. This means that there are many people living in a small space. In the capital of Taipei, there were 25,225 people for every square mile of land (9,737 people per square kilometer).

Taiwanese people are friendly, respectful of others, and do not like loud, unrefined behavior. They value patience and are very hard working. A survey conducted in 2001 showed that Taiwanese people worked an average of 53.4 hours per week, compared to the 42.4 hours per week worked by Americans. Children in Taiwan study extremely hard. When Taiwanese find time to relax, the most popular recreational activities are walking, cycling, jogging, hiking, and playing basketball.

AIR POLLUTION

The exhaust fumes of the many vehicles and the large number of industrial factories in Taiwan have resulted in a serious air pollution problem.

(A Closer Look, page 46)

Family Life

Above: **Although most families in Taiwan are small, many families live in crowded conditions as a result of the high population density in the country. Small families allow parents to spend more time with their children. Taiwanese parents often take their children on excursions to visit the country's attractions.**

The modern Taiwanese family is small and usually has only one or two children. In Taiwan, however, a family is made up of children, parents, and extended family members. In rural areas, it is still common to find several generations of a family living together. This once was the practice all over Taiwan, but today, young people living in cities usually live separately from their families.

In the family, the father is the authority figure. His main duty, however, lies in being a good son to his own parents. His wife and children come second to his duty to his parents. Women are traditionally responsible for raising children, although family members, such as grandparents, may assist with this job. A wife becomes part of her husband's family and would show greater loyalty to her husband and his parents than to the family into which she was born.

Ideas on the role of women in the family have rapidly changed over the last few decades in Taiwan. In fact, family structures in Taiwan have also changed. As people move from rural areas to the cities, more women have started to work outside the home, and they have become influenced by Western ideas.

Men are no longer seen as the only breadwinners of families, and women have far more choices available to them. Contact with extended family members has decreased.

The divorce rate in Taiwan has reached a new high—about six times the rate of thirty years ago. Women have gained increased independence by working outside the home, and this has given them the money and freedom to end unhappy marriages. There is, however, still a slight stigma attached to being a divorced women.

Many traditional values are still important in Taiwan today. One example is that younger family members must show respect for their elders. This extends even to deceased family members. Ancestors are remembered in many ways. For example, places are set at the table for ancestors when the family celebrates the New Year.

Another traditional aspect of Taiwanese family life is that "losing face" is to be avoided at all costs. In other words, how the family is viewed by others in society is very important. Many Taiwanese families keep their conflicts secret rather than face the embarrassment of having others know about them. The way a family is perceived is so important that if one member acts inappropriately, it affects the reputation of all family members and makes them lose face, or become ashamed.

Below: **These retired gentlemen gather at a park in the city of Taipei to chat with friends. In Taiwan, older people are treated with great respect by the young.**

Education

The literacy rate in Taiwan is high. Schooling is compulsory for Taiwanese from the age of six until the age of fifteen. Preschool is not compulsory. More and more parents, however, are sending their children to preschool for one or two years in order to help them succeed in the competitive Taiwanese educational system.

In elementary school, students study languages, health and physical education, social studies, arts, mathematics, nature, and technology. English lessons are compulsory beginning in fifth grade. A Taiwanese dialect, such as Southern Fujianese, Hakka, or one of the aboriginal dialects, is studied from first through sixth grades. In junior high school, this second language is optional.

Graduation to the next level of schooling in Taiwan has traditionally been based on examinations. These examinations determine if students qualify to attend either senior high school or senior vocational school. Senior high school prepares students for further university or college study. Senior vocational schools, on the other hand, prepare students for work in specialized areas

Below: **Taiwanese school children lead active lives. Some students even join the Boy Scouts or Girl Guides, where they learn practical skills such as first aid.**

such as art, music, agriculture, and nursing. Both of these are three-year programs. The government introduced alternative ways for students to pass from junior high school to the next level in 1996. Most students, however, still take the examinations.

Gifted students and students with special needs due to disabilities attend special schools. These special schools are run for students of elementary through senior-high-school levels.

Because there are more students than there are university places in Taiwan, entrance to the country's universities is extremely competitive. Most students who plan to go to college spend a year preparing for the university entrance examinations by memorizing huge amounts of information. These students often attend school during normal hours and then attend test preparation classes after school.

As an alternative to entering a university, students can study at junior colleges. Courses at junior colleges last for two years and cover specialized areas such as business, forestry, engineering, and home economics. Some students attend junior college and then go on to obtain a university degree.

Above: **Taiwan's first university was established in Taipei in 1928 by the Japanese government during its occupation of Taiwan. The university name was changed to National Taiwan University in 1946.**

TAIWANESE TEMPLES

The Lung Shan Temple (*left*) in Taipei is one of the most popular temples in the country. While Taiwan still has some purely Buddhist temples, most people practice a combination of Buddhism, Taoism, and folk religion in one temple.

(A Closer Look, page 68)

Religion

The main religions in Taiwan are Buddhism, Taoism, and Confucianism. Taoists and Buddhists used to worship separately. When the Japanese occupied Taiwan from 1895 to 1945, the Taoists were persecuted, and they began worshiping secretly in Buddhist temples. By the time Taiwan returned to Chinese administration after World War II, the two religions had blended together.

Taoism is a Chinese religion that encourages individual freedom. Even when the religion was first practiced in China, it was mixed with Buddhism and folk religion.

Buddhism originated in India and is based on the teachings of Gautama Buddha, an Indian prince who chose a simple way of life. By living simply and meditating for long periods of time, he achieved a state of mind called enlightenment. His followers also attempt to achieve this state of mind. Buddhism came to Taiwan from China in the seventeenth century.

Most people do not see Confucianism as a religion but as a way of living. Confucius lived 2,500 years ago, and his teachings

***Above:* This monk dressed in traditional robes begs for alms along a street in Taipei.**

on morals have been passed from generation to generation. His teachings promote ancestor worship and reverence toward heaven. Every year, on September 28, Confucius's birthday is celebrated in Taipei at a temple built to honor him.

Chinese immigrants also brought with them a variety of folk beliefs, images of gods, and objects of worship that are not used in Buddhism and Taoism. Some believe, for example, that the head of all gods is called the God of Heaven, and that underneath this figure are other gods who can be called on for special needs.

When visiting a Taoist temple, some Taiwanese perform folk rituals to seek help from the gods. In one ritual, people burn three sticks of incense in front of an altar. In their own minds, they repeat their name, birth date, and address, and then state the question they would like answered. They then drop two wooden blocks shaped like half-moons. If the blocks land on opposite ends, the answer is positive. If both curved sides land facing up, the answer is negative. If both blocks land with the flat side up, the person tries again.

Christianity was introduced to Taiwan in the early seventeenth century by Spanish and Dutch missionaries. There are still a few Protestant and Catholic churches in Taiwan today.

FENG SHUI

Many Taiwanese practice the ancient art of feng shui, which is based on a set of principles that claim that a person's well-being can be enhanced by the way their home or office is arranged.

(A Closer Look, page 54)

Below: A number of Christians live in Taiwan today. This church choir in Taipei performs as part of a worship service.

Language and Literature

The national language of Taiwan is Mandarin, which is the Chinese dialect that originated from Beijing, China, over 1,000 years ago. The people of each region of Taiwan speak slightly different versions of Mandarin that reflect the influence of the native dialects of the areas.

Taiwanese Mandarin has developed to such an extent that it has become distinguishable from the Mandarin spoken in China. The characteristics of Taiwanese Mandarin have been greatly influenced by the dialect known as Southern Fujianese. Southern Fujianese is spoken fluently by up to 70 percent of Taiwanese, but because of the pressure to adopt the national language, this dialect has taken a backseat for a long time.

Although many aborigines are bilingual, some of them who have come to work in the cities have lost touch with their native dialects. The government has tried to encourage aboriginal cultural events and radio programs to revive some dialects that are at risk of dying out. The government also provides special language education for native aborigines.

Above: **Although Taiwanese signs are often written in Chinese and English, the English translation may not be what a native English speaker is used to seeing.**

Left: **Taiwan has a literacy rate of over 94 percent. Sometimes, general interest news and bulletins are put up on notice boards in parks and other public areas for the convenience of the older people who otherwise may not have access to the information.**

Left: **This woman teaches her son the proper way to write Mandarin characters. In Taiwan, Mandarin is written in a vertical line from top to bottom. The Mandarin language is read from right to left, unlike English, which is read from left to right.**

Literature

Many Chinese intellectuals arrived in Taiwan from the 1600s to the 1800s. Shen Kuang-wen, who came to Taiwan in 1662, helped form a Taiwanese poets' society and introduce classical Chinese literature in Taiwan. His poetry mainly spoke about patriotism and sadness at the loss of the Chinese Ming Empire.

At the start of the Japanese occupation in 1895, famous writers were still writing in classical Chinese. By the 1920s, the Taiwanese New Literature movement encouraged the writing of literature in several languages, including Southern Fujianese and Japanese. Initially, writers resisted Japanese colonial rule, but, later, a new generation of writers who were less critical of the Japanese colonization of Taiwan emerged. These writers, however, came to resent Japanese rule in Taiwan when the government tightened restrictions during World War II.

In the 1950s, during the rule of Chiang Kai-shek, revolutionary writing was suppressed, and lyrical works were popular. Anti-communist works were also widespread.

Literature in Taiwan in recent times has been influenced by foreign cultures and modernization. Instead of politics, writers have explored topics reflecting the newer, wealthier Taiwan.

Arts

Taiwan's aboriginal cultures provide the country with a rich variety of art forms. Each group of aborigines has developed its own style of art, music, and dance. Wood carving, weaving, and basketry are common aboriginal art forms. Ceremonial music and dance have also been an important part of aboriginal life over the centuries.

Wood Carvings

The wood carvings of the Paiwan and Rukai aboriginal peoples are well known. Important people, such as leaders in these aboriginal groups, usually decorate their homes with wood carvings depicting zigzag patterns, humans, and a snake design with a diamond-shaped head. The snake represents the reincarnation, or rebirth, of ancestors.

Weaving and Other Crafts

The Atayal aborigines are known for their beautiful weavings made using simple looms. Strings of thin shell beads and rows of tiny bronze bells are sometimes incorporated into their designs.

Below: **The aboriginal people are highly skilled in wood carving. This shop displays statues of the Buddha in different poses.**

Typical patterns involve triangles, squares, and diamonds, and the predominant colors are white, red, blue, and black.

Chinese folk arts, including dough sculpture, knotting, and paper cutting, are still popular. Performances of dragon and lion dances, puppet shows, folk dances, and operas are also common.

Dance and Music

In all the aboriginal groups, the richest traditions involve dance and music. Dances are usually performed at ceremonies and accompanied by tuneful singing. The dance steps are simple and often involve walking and foot stomping. Dancers wear bright, colorful costumes. Small bells and metal ornaments that jingle during dancing can be attached to dancers'costumes.

Aboriginal music reflects all aspects of tribal life, including harvests, daily work, love, and tribal legends. Aboriginal musical instruments include simple stringed instruments, drums, flutelike woodwind instruments, and percussion instruments, such as rattles.

Above: **Taiwanese enjoy listening to music. Many people learn to play a musical instrument when they are in school. They may also join a band that performs at parades and functions.**

Modern Arts

Puppet shows were hugely popular in Taiwan before the arrival of television in the 1960s. These shows usually took place at festive events such as weddings, holidays, and temple festivals. Puppet troupes traveled from village to village on foot with their puppet shows, carrying their stage, musical instruments, and cases on poles over their shoulders. Although the art form has been enhanced with modern innovations, puppets have kept their traditional characteristics.

Dragon dances are performed during celebrations like the New Year Festival. The dragon dance is performed by a line of between nine and twenty-five dancers. The first dancer wears a large dragon's-head mask, while the others carry sections of the body that are covered in gold, green, or red fabric. They dance in such a way that, together, they look like a single twisting, turning dragon.

Taiwan is famous for its opera, and performances take place at opera schools across the country. Community theaters and temples also put on shows, and operas are broadcast on television. Taiwanese opera and Chinese opera are the two most common styles performed. Chinese opera is usually sung in the Chinese dialect of the region from which the opera originated. Taiwanese opera is performed in Southern Fujianese.

Woodblock printing is a traditional art form that has become popular again. Images are carved into wood and printed in black on red or orange paper. The outlines are then filled in with other colors. Lunar New Year hangings are made in this way. These colorful prints originate from mainland China's Fujian Province, the original home of some of Taiwan's immigrants. Prints often feature the gods of Taiwanese folklore, such as the God of Wealth, the Kitchen God, and the Door Gods. These gods are drawn wearing elaborate clothing and have fierce-looking faces.

Temples are another important part of the art world in Taiwan, as they often host events such as lantern-making competitions, puppet shows, and folk operas. Temples are also the homes of traditional crafts such as stone carvings, ceramic figures, and intricate embroidered banners. Wood carvings can be seen in abundance at most temples. The structure of the temple is often made of wood, and its beams are often carved with legendary figures from history and folklore. Pictures of birds, dragons, and mythical creatures can also be seen in wood carvings.

OPERA PERFORMANCES

Watching opera is a popular pastime for the Taiwanese. In Chinese opera (*above*), performers often wear elaborate costumes and heavy makeup.
(A Closer Look, page 58)

PUPPETRY

An important aspect of Taiwanese culture is puppetry, as it plays a role in religious worship and folk festivals. Glove puppets, shadow puppets, and marionettes are the most common styles.
(A Closer Look, page 63)

Opposite: Lion dance performers dressed in their costumes. The lion dance is supposed to bring good luck and is often performed at New Year festivals and auspicious events, such as the openings of new shops.

Leisure and Festivals

Traditional Games

Many of the games played in Taiwan are traditional Chinese folk games. For example, a game called *diabolo* (di-a-BOH-loh) is played by both young and old. A wooden object called a diabolo, which is shaped like a barbell, is balanced on a string that is tied between two sticks. A player holds the sticks, allowing the diabolo to spin as it rolls along the string. The diabolo can be thrown into the air and caught again on the string while it is still spinning. When the diabolo is spinning quickly, it makes a humming sound.

Played mostly by children, top spinning is another traditional Chinese game that is popular in Taiwan. The tops are made of wood, metal, or plastic and come in all sizes. It is particularly impressive to see a giant-size top being spun. This trick, however, is usually performed only by adults.

Shuttlecock kicking is another folk game originating in China. It can be done even in a very small area. Sometimes, two people

Below: **Kite flying is a traditional sport still popular in Taiwan today. The Taipei County International Kites Festival attracts thousands of enthusiasts.**

Left: **One of the favorite pastimes of the Taiwanese people is watching movies. Other activities that they enjoy are going on picnics, listening to music, and hiking.**

will play, kicking a shuttlecock back and forth between them. Just as tricks can be performed with soccer balls, shuttlecock kicking can also become very advanced. It is a great form of exercise.

Jumping rope is another fantastic form of exercise popular with children in Taiwan. It is most often done outdoors in large groups. Children jump alone with a shorter rope or jump over a larger rope with several people together.

Hobbies

Traveling overseas is extremely popular among Taiwanese people. The government has been trying to encourage people to travel within Taiwan. Sports and recreation centers have been established to motivate Taiwanese to vacation in the country.

Since Taiwan is a technologically advanced nation, watching television, playing computer games, Web surfing, and Internet chat rooms are all popular activities. Over half of the teenagers in Taiwan have visited an Internet café. Even so, the peace and harmony of the outdoors appeal to the people. If you visit a park in a city like Taipei, you will see people walking and jogging, practicing martial arts such as taijiquan, and playing Chinese chess, which is similar to Western chess.

TAIJIQUAN

A traditional Chinese martial art, *taijiquan* (TY-chee-choo-en) is practiced by people of all ages in Taiwan.

(A Closer Look, page 64)

Sports

Taiwanese children are introduced to sports while in school, where they attend complusory physical education classes. Although the education system places more importance on academic studies than sports, most students learn to play a variety of sports including baseball, martial arts, softball, and volleyball. When the children leave school, practicing sports can be expensive as sporting facilities are hard to come by in crowded cities. For adults, the most popular recreational sports in Taiwan are walking, cycling, basketball, jogging, and hiking.

Taiwanese athletes excel in dragon boat racing. This sport originated from a festival commemorating the death of a Chinese poet, Chu Yuan. Now, the sport takes place in countries around the world and international dragon boat races are held in Taipei. Martial arts such as judo, tae kwon do, and kendo are also popular in Taiwan. International championships take place regularly between Asian countries, in competitions such as the Asian Games. Surfing, scuba diving, and sailboarding are popular on the shores of the island. In addition, newer sports, such as rollerblading, are becoming popular in Taiwan.

Above: **Huge stadiums such as this one play host to many sporting events. One of the most popular sports is baseball. In 2002, during the thirteenth season of the Chinese Professional Baseball League, games attracted an average of 3,500 fans.**

Baseball

Baseball was introduced to Taiwan in the late nineteenth century. Today, Little League is offered to girls and boys in about half of Taiwan's elementary and junior high schools. A popular spectator sport, baseball reached its peak in Taiwan in 1996 when games were played in near sell-out stadiums. In 1997, a corruption scandal led to the departure of well-known players and interest in the game dropped. In early 2003, Taiwan's two baseball leagues merged into one league with six teams and tried to win back fans.

Taiwan in the Olympics

Taiwan was initially not able to independently compete in the Olympic Games because mainland China claimed that Taiwan was also part of China. In 1958, mainland China withdrew from Olympic competition, and Taiwan competed under the name "China" in the 1960, 1964, 1968, and 1972 games. In 1976, Taiwan withdrew after the International Olympic Committee (IOC) ruled that it could not compete under that name. The IOC recognized the Olympic committee from mainland China in 1979. In 1981, the IOC and Taiwan came to an agreement, and since 1984, Taiwan has competed under the name "Chinese Taipei."

Left: **Yang Chuan-kwang *(right)* is perhaps the most famous Taiwanese athlete of all time. A member of the Ami aboriginal tribe, Yang won a silver medal in the decathlon at the 1960 Rome Olympics.**

Festivals

Many festivals in Taiwan recognize important events in Chinese history. Other festivals reflect the people's devotion to folk gods, the spirits of dead ancestors, and heroes. As most festivals in Taiwan fall on a fixed day on the lunar calendar—that is, based on the motion of the moon—celebration dates vary each year.

The first major festival of the year is the Lunar New Year, sometimes also called the Chinese New Year. It lasts for fifteen days, and it is a time for families to come together. Offerings are made to gods and people are very superstitious around this time. The festival concludes with the decorative celebrations of the Lantern Festival on the first full moon of the lunar calendar.

The birthday of the Earth Gods and the Medicine God are celebrated early in the year. Legend has it that the Earth Gods were once like tax collectors. Every place is guarded by its own earth god. On his birthday, people worship in temples from dawn until noon. The Medicine God was once a human healer named Wu Pen. To celebrate his birthday, stilt walkers and bands perform in an elaborate procession.

LUNAR NEW YEAR FESTIVAL

This festival has many traditions that require much preparation, but people are happy to follow the customs, as it is a time for them to spend time with family members whom they seldom get to see.
(A Closer Look, page 56)

Left: **Participants in a parade celebrating the Double Tenth National Day in Taipei hold up posters of Sun Yat Sen, who is considered a hero in Taiwan.**

Above: **Festivals are often happy times for people. During this festival, which celebrates a folk belief, street performers wear colorful costumes and masks and entertain the public with their songs and dances.**

One of the biggest festivals is the birthday of Matsu (MAH-tsoo), the goddess of the sea, in the third lunar month. A legend says that Matsu rescued her father, brother, and other fishermen from drowning, even though she was at home. Rituals in her honor take place at temples throughout Taiwan on her birthday.

Soon after Matsu's birthday comes the annual Dragon Boat Festival. During this festival, dragon boat races take place in the country's major rivers. Teams from around the world compete in these famous races. Special rice dumplings wrapped in bamboo leaves are eaten in honor of scholar and statesman Chu Yuan, who drowned during this festival in ancient Chinese times.

The next major festival in the calendar is the Ghost Festival, held in the seventh lunar month. At this time, it is believed that the gates of Hell open, and spirits visit the land of the living. Elaborate temple ceremonies are held and feasts are provided for the ghosts.

In mid-fall, the Mid-Autumn Festival celebrates the harvest moon. Families reunite and eat rich pastries called mooncakes while appreciating the full moon.

Double Tenth National Day commemorates the anniversary of the revolution that overthrew the Ching dynasty in China on October 10, 1911.

Food

Mealtime is an important part of family life in Taiwan. Both when guests are present and at everyday family gatherings, meals include a variety of food. Once every one has gathered, the main dish is placed in the middle of the table, and each person then serves food from this central dish into his or her rice bowl.

Taiwanese use chopsticks and soup spoons for eating utensils. While most people are not too particular about dining etiquette, there are some general guidelines. For example, it is rude to place your chopsticks pointing straight up out of the dish, as this is a symbol of death. Also, if there is a guest of honor at the meal, she or he should eat before anyone else can begin.

When dining at a restaurant in Taiwan, the level of noise can be quite surprising. This is because dining out is considered a joyous occasion for the Taiwanese. The bigger the group, the merrier is the gathering, and the louder is the noise!

Soups and seafood, pork, chicken, and vegetable dishes are all common in Taiwan. Many dishes are prepared by stir-frying and are usually accompanied by rice. Tea is often served, too.

Below: **In Taiwan, there are many streetside stalls that sell a variety of sweet desserts. Make a selection from the ingredients available, and the shopkeeper will add shaved ice and syrup for a delicious cold snack.**

Left: The restaurant business is very competitive in Taiwan. Most shops will set up display counters to attract passersby to drop in and try their food. This shop sells a variety of stir-fried dishes.

Taiwan's food has strong Chinese influences. Each region of mainland China has its own distinctive cuisine, and these regional specialties arrived in Taiwan with Chinese immigrants. Two popular types of Chinese food in Taiwan are Sichuan cuisine and Hunan cuisine. These foods are rich in garlic, scallions, and chilies. Sichuan food has a hot, peppery taste. Hunan food, on the other hand, is rich and can be either hot and spicy or sweet and sour.

Cantonese cuisine, popular in Western countries, is also available in Taiwan. Its dishes are colorful and slightly less spicy than other types of Chinese food.

Taiwanese cuisine is light, and it emphasizes natural flavors and the freshness of ingredients. The food is relatively easy to prepare and is often flavored with ginger. In contrast, Hakka food has heavier flavors and often features fried, spicy, well-done, salty, and fatty dishes. Tonic foods, or dishes that include some form of medicinal ingredients or herbs, are also often prepared in Taiwan.

Some popular dishes in Taiwan are deep-fried bean curd, pig-blood cake, vermicelli noodles with intestines, deep-fried chicken parts, fried onion pancake, and rice with soy-sauce stewed pork.

TEA DRINKING

Serious tea drinkers will tell you that there is an art to tea brewing and drinking. Many shops in Taipei offer a selection of tea leaves for making this popular beverage.

(A Closer Look, page 70)

慶祝中華民國國慶

A CLOSER LOOK AT TAIWAN

Taiwan is today regarded as an industrialized country and its people enjoy a high standard of living. The country is well known as one of the world's largest producers of electronic components, electrical appliances, and mobile phones. While many people are familiar with the country's success in these fields, not very much is widely known about Taiwan's people, history, or rich culture.

Because the majority of Taiwanese people are of Chinese origin, the country's festivals, practices, customs, and language are fairly similar to those of other Chinese communities. There are, however, subtle differences that set Taiwan apart from the rest of the world.

Below: **Taiwan is an advanced nation and teenagers in the country are well informed about what is happening around the world.**

One example is the country's written language. The Taiwanese use traditional Chinese characters, while many other Chinese communities have switched to using simplified Chinese characters.

Taiwan and mainland China have had a rocky relationship since 1949, when the communists won the mainland and the Kuomintang took tighter control of Taiwan. Although the United States and Canada do not have formal diplomatic relations with Taiwan, there is a great deal of trade between North America and Taiwan. The U.S has also pledged to protect Taiwan from any threat from China.

Opposite: **Cheerleaders with pom-poms wait for their turn to perform during the Double Tenth celebrations in Taipei.**

Aborigines and Hakkas

The aboriginal people of Taiwan have lived on the island for thousands of years. Eleven of the original aboriginal tribes remain today. These are the Ami, Atayal, Bunun, Kavalan, Paiwan, Puyuma, Rukai, Saisiyat, Thao, Tsou, and Yami people.

Many aborigines live in government-designated areas in the mountains of central and southern Taiwan. Other aborigines, however, have moved to the cities, where they speak Mandarin rather than their aboriginal dialects. Because of this, it is hard for aborigines to keep their culture alive. The tradition of passing down stories from generation to generation is in great danger. Recently, some of their stories have been printed so that young aborigines can learn about their tribes' history and stories.

Before the arrival of the Hakka people in Taiwan, the aborigines had the entire land to themselves. When the Hakkas, meaning "guest people," arrived, the newcomers pushed the aborigines into the mountains in order to keep the fertile coastal lands for themselves.

Above: **It is common among older aboriginal women to have their faces painted in traditional patterns.**

Left: **Female aborigines wear brightly colored costumes and necklaces. They sometimes also wear fancy headdresses.**

Above: **In an effort to preserve their heritage, Taiwan's aborigines often stage traditional dance performances, such as this one at the Taiwan Aboriginal Culture Park.**

Although there is some dispute about the origins of the Hakka people, it seems that they were a persecuted minority in China. Their facial features made them look different from other Chinese, which led to their being referred to as *hakkas* (HAK-kars), or guests, and this name stuck. The Hakkas were driven from their homes in northern China and migrated further and further south before coming to Taiwan. Although these people originated in northern China, their language was influenced by the language of people from the south.

When other groups of immigrants arrived in Taiwan from China, they forced the Hakkas into the mountains. The newly arrived Chinese immigrants called themselves *ben di ren* (BUHN dee ren), meaning "people of this place," to distinguish themselves from the Hakkas and the aborigines. Most of today's Taiwanese people are descendants of the ben di ren.

While there are several million Hakka people in Taiwan today, very few speak the Hakka language. Most Hakkas have grown up speaking Southern Fujianese and Mandarin. Just as there are programs to teach young aborigines their native languages and traditions, there are similar programs for Hakkas.

Air Pollution

One of the most serious environmental problems in Taiwan is the air pollution that is mainly caused by the country's heavy traffic and high number of industrial plants. In 2000, it was reported that there were 2.76 factories and 445 vehicles for every 0.386 square mile (1 square km) of land in Taiwan. In 2001, 17.4 million vehicles (5.7 million cars and 11.7 million motorbikes) were registered in Taiwan—nearly three vehicles for every four people—and the number is expected to continue growing.

In Taipei, air pollution is mostly caused by the exhaust fumes from traffic. Motorbikes and scooters are the main form of transportation in Taipei. The exhaust fumes from city traffic are so thick that people sometimes wear masks over their mouths while riding their motorbikes.

Air pollution in Taipei is made worse by the city's location. The mountains surrounding the city create a "bowl" that traps air pollution. Other cities in Taiwan that have a lot of air pollution are located on the coast, so they do not have the same problem.

Below: **Traffic in the city of Taipei is very heavy. Exhaust from vehicles stuck in traffic jams adds to the pollution problem.**

Left: **The growth of the industrial sector in Taiwan has resulted in the building of more factories. These factories often consume vast amounts of energy, further aggravating the country's pollution problem.**

Taiwan's Environmental Protection Administration (EPA) has tried to reduce the harmful impact of motor vehicles on air pollution. In 1999, it began paying people who reported cars and motorbikes that were giving off especially large amounts of dark smoke. The EPA also offered a U.S. $1,000 grant to people who bought exhaust-free electric motorbikes.

When a country uses energy in forms such as electricity and natural gas, it causes air pollution. The amount of energy used in Taiwan is on par with several of its neighboring countries in Asia. Taiwanese people, however, use five times more energy per capita than Chinese people. With the growth of the Taiwanese economy, energy use in Taiwan has more than doubled since 1980.

It is not just electricity and natural gas that are used in Taiwan. Since 1980, nuclear and hydroelectric sources of energy have been developed. These sources of energy do not release carbon into the environment and, therefore, do not add to the air pollution problem.

民主
倫理

Chiang Kai-shek

Born in China's Zhejiang Province on October 31, 1887, Chiang Kai-shek studied Chinese classics, current affairs, and Western law at school. After completing school, Chiang trained with the Japanese army. In 1911, Chiang returned to China and joined the revolutionary movement seeking to overthrow the Ching rulers. He became Sun Yat Sen's military aide in 1918. Later, he was commandant of Whampoa Military Academy.

By the time Sun Yat Sen died in 1925, Chiang had become an important figure in the Kuomintang army. In 1926, he led the Kuomintang army in the Northern Expedition. Chiang began a civil war against the Communists in 1927, and by the end of 1927, he was head of China's Kuomintang government.

During World War II, Chiang was considered China's leader, representing the country during international peace talks. The civil war, however, continued after World War II ended. In 1949, Chiang was forced to flee to Taiwan, reestablishing the Kuomintang in Taiwan, with himself as president.

Chiang's rule of Taiwan was seen as a dictatorship. The people had no freedom of expression as criticism of the government was not allowed. Chiang did, however, provide for their welfare. He encouraged economic development, improved the education system, and secured a defense agreement with the United States. When Chiang took over Taiwan, the country's economy was in shambles. During his rule, Taiwan received economic aid from the U.S., which was used to rebuild the country and help the agricultural sector. This was successful, and by 1959, 90 percent of Taiwan's exports were agriculturally related.

In the early 1950s, the government introduced a policy to make Taiwan self-sufficient. Factories made inexpensive consumer goods and fewer items were imported. A second policy in the late 1950s established special trade zones and tax incentives to attract overseas investment. From 1962 to 1985, Taiwan's economy witnessed an annual economic growth rate of nearly 10 percent.

Despite Taiwan's rapid economic development under Chiang, the United Nations decided to recognize the Communists as the true government of China in 1971. On April 5, 1975, Chiang died in Taiwan without realizing his dream of ruling a united China.

Above: **As the ruler of Taiwan, Chiang Kai-shek was successful in modernizing the country. The policies he implemented in the 1950s laid the foundation for Taiwan's economic growth in later years.**

Opposite: **The Chiang Kai-shek Memorial Hall in Taipei is a popular attraction for both locals and tourists who wish to learn about Taiwan's history**

Early European Contact

Before the fifteenth century, the trip from Europe to Asia involved a long trek over land. When the sea route between Europe and Asia was finally discovered, the journey became a lot simpler. In the sixteenth century, countries such as Spain, Portugal, Holland, France, and England all wanted to increase their power by finding as many trade routes and establishing as many colonies in Asia as possible.

Above: **Fort San Domingo, located in the town of Tanshui north of Taipei, is one of the legacies of the European occupation of Taiwan.**

Portugal was one of the first European nations to explore sea routes to Asia and is credited as the first Western nation to take note of Taiwan. Sailors in the 1590s, called the island "Ilha Formosa" and the natives "Formosans," meaning "beautiful people." From this time on, many Europeans learned of Taiwan and wanted to seize the island. One reason for this was Taiwan's convenient position between northern and southeast Asia. Taiwan was also well positioned for countries that wanted to trade with China. The Ching government in China, however, did not allow its people to trade with Europeans. Taiwan was the best base for the Europeans while they attempted to get around this restriction.

The Dutch eventually occupied southwest Taiwan. In 1624, they arrived in what is now the region surrounding Tainan. The Dutch used local Chinese labor to build churches and forts, and they imposed heavy taxes on the island's population to fund these projects. A number of Dutch missionaries also tried to convert the people living in Taiwan to Christianity.

In 1626, Spain occupied Chi-Lung and Tanshui in the north. From northern Taiwan, the Spanish tried to develop trade with China and Japan, but they were not successful.

***Below:* Christianity was introduced to Taiwan by European settlers. The religion is still practiced in Taiwan today, and churches can be found throughout the country.**

By 1641, the Dutch tried to force the Spanish out, and the Spanish eventually decided to leave Taiwan. The Dutch remained in control of Taiwan for thirty-seven years. In 1661, Chinese-born Cheng Cheng-kung arrived on the island and began his siege against the Dutch. After two years, the Dutch finally left, and Cheng became a national hero.

European influence dating from these years is still apparent in parts of Taiwan. A few Christian churches, established by both Dutch and Spanish missionaries, still exist in the country today.

The Electronics Industry

Taiwan is famous for its electronics manufacturing industry, which has been developing over the last forty years.

During the 1960s, the electronics industry was in its infancy. At that time, the main electronic goods made by Taiwanese companies were transistor radios and tape recorders. In the early 1970s, however, the Taiwanese government made a decision to change and promote the electronics industry. During the 1970s, Taiwan initially manufactured electronic components, or parts, that were exported to other countries for assembly.

By the 1980s, electronics had become Taiwan's biggest export, and Taiwanese companies began manufacturing complete products such as color monitors and computers. Taiwan also started to make semiconductors, or materials that conduct electricity well at high temperatures but do not conduct well at low temperatures, in the 1980s. These materials are used in many products, including railway switches and computer parts.

Below: **These Taiwanese women work on a production line in a factory that manufactures semiconductors. Semiconductors are used in a variety of products, including communication devices.**

Above: **A visitor to one of Taiwan's leading electronics companies in the city of Taipei checks out a wall of monitors showing the production line. Since the government made an effort to develop the electronics industry, the country has become extremely successful.**

In the 1990s, microelectronics manufacturing grew in Taiwan. Taiwanese companies became the world's biggest suppliers of motherboards, monitors, scanners, and mice. By 1995, Taiwan had become one of the biggest suppliers of computers in the world. Some Taiwanese computer companies, such as Acer, produce under their own brand name. Most others, however, act as manufacturers and suppliers of computer parts to leading companies such as Apple, Compaq, IBM, NEC, and Twinhead.

Some of Taiwan's exports have stayed the same over the years. For example, semiconductors are still one of Taiwan's biggest exports. In fact, in 2001, Taiwan was ranked the fourth largest producer of semiconductors in the world. It was also the second largest maker of TFT (thin-film transistor) LCDs. Among the newer products starting to be produced in large quantities in Taiwan are digital cameras and PDAs (personal digital assistants).

The electronics industry in Taiwan looks set to continue to grow, and Taiwan will probably be the supplier of new technologies as they are developed.

Feng Shui

The ancient Chinese practice of feng shui has been around for several thousand years, and it is still used in Taiwan today. Feng shui is a method of placing objects within a house and even determining the placement of graves, temples, and other buildings in a city. The Chinese believe that *chi* (CHEE), or energy, exists within humans. They also believe chi comes from Earth and the universe. Feng shui principles deal with how one's surroundings and their chi affect people. The practice of feng shui is supposed to help people organize their objects, furniture, and houses in the way that best harnesses Earth's forces and powers so that good fortune and prosperity will come; it is a way of ensuring harmony and balance.

Many people follow feng shui principles to ensure a smooth flow of energy through their houses. General examples of good feng shui practices are easy to state. For example, wind chimes should be placed near fans and air conditioners to enliven the chi of a house. In the kitchen, the refrigerator and the oven should

Below: The office of this feng shui master follows the principles of good feng shui. Plants are placed on the desk and in the bookshelf to counter negative energy. The desk has probably been arranged to face the correct point to ensure that the person using it is successful in business.

not face each other directly, or the opposing forces of heat and cold will clash. In the dining room, there should be an even number of chairs. An odd number of chairs means that there is a single chair is left out of a pair; this represents loneliness. Curves are believed to create harmony, whereas sharp corners are a bad omen. A believer in feng shui, thus, will never buy a house built on land that is shaped like a triangle. Sharp corners in an office are said to drive away money, so rounded corners are preferred on desks and counters. Feng shui practitioners, however, say that feng shui is not as simple as merely following rules, because each environment is different.

Feng shui was originally only practiced by a small group of masters for the ruling class in China. During the Tang dynasty (A.D. 618-906) of China, Yang Yun-sang wrote books that outlined the principles of feng shui. It was the arrival of Chiang Kai-shek in Taiwan in 1949 that signalled the introduction of feng shui to the island. Many of Chiang's followers who came with him brought with them valuable old feng shui texts, making the art more accessible.

Above: **According to feng shui principles, some days are luckier than others. These lucky days are the best times to start new businesses. Inviting lion dancers to perform at a business opening on a lucky day is believed to bring even more good luck.**

Lunar New Year Festival

The most important festival celebrated in Taiwan is the Lunar New Year, also known as the Spring Festival. This festival begins on the first day of a new lunar year, which usually falls in either January or February, and lasts for fifteen days.

Trains, buses, and planes around the country are fully booked in the days before the festival, as people travel to be with their families. Shops close for one week, and even the traffic congestion in Taipei clears. While some people use this break to go on family vacations overseas, many families remain in the country to celebrate the age-old Chinese traditions that form part of the festival. Superstitions abound at this time. Conflict is seen as extremely unlucky, so quarrels are avoided. Floors are not swept and garbage is not thrown out, for fear of sweeping away or disposing of riches.

On New Year's Eve, a lavish family meal is shared and places are set at the table for ancestors. The food served is symbolic of good luck. For example, the Chinese word for fish, *yu* (YOO),

Below: **In the weeks leading up to the New Year Festival, shops sell special decorations for homes and offices. These include paper lanterns, paper cutouts, and couplets written on red paper. The color red is considered lucky by the Chinese.**

is a homonym for abundance. The family usually stays awake all night. Traditionally, the Chinese believed that doing so would allow their parents to live a long life. It is also a good way to make the most of the rare occasion when the whole family is together. Legend has it that a fierce beast called Nien goes around eating people on New Year's Eve. As Nien is said to fear light and loud noise, the sound of firecrackers is heard throughout the night.

On New Year's Day in Taiwan, new clothes are worn to symbolize a fresh beginning. Offerings are made to ancestors and respect is paid to the gods. Younger family members also pay respect to living elders. Visits are made to friends to exchange good wishes, and dragon and lion dances are performed.

From the fifth day onward, shops reopen, and the festival begins to wind down. The Lantern Festival, which takes place two weeks after New Year's Eve, brings the festival to a close. Temples are decorated with beautiful lanterns at this time, and families prepare rice dumplings called *tang yuan* (TUHNG yuen). These round dumplings symbolize family unity. Today, fireworks and riddle-guessing contests have been incorporated into the activities of the lively Lantern Festival.

Above: **Children are especially happy during the New Year Festival because they are given red envelopes, called *hong pau* (hon POW), that contain "lucky money." Hong pau are usually given by married people.**

Opera Performances

One major traditional form of entertainment in Taiwan is Chinese opera. Over the years, adaptations of the original Chinese opera style have created a style known as Taiwanese opera.

Although Chinese opera performances are not held as frequently as in the past, they can still be seen on a weekly basis in Taipei's theaters. Several well-known troupes, as well as many amateur groups, perform Chinese opera in Taiwan. People can also watch Chinese operas on television or listen to performances on radio.

A Chinese opera stage usually has a beautiful embroidered backdrop. The singers enter the stage to the music of stringed and woodwind instruments or the sounds of gongs and drums. Chinese opera plots are based on historical stories or folklore legends. The shows are either tragic or funny. Performances can involve singing, dancing, and poetry. Chinese opera choreography involves extremely difficult movements. Sometimes their costumes make the characters' movements even more

***Below:* Performers in Chinese and Taiwanese opera are often heavily made-up and wear elaborate costumes and headdresses.**

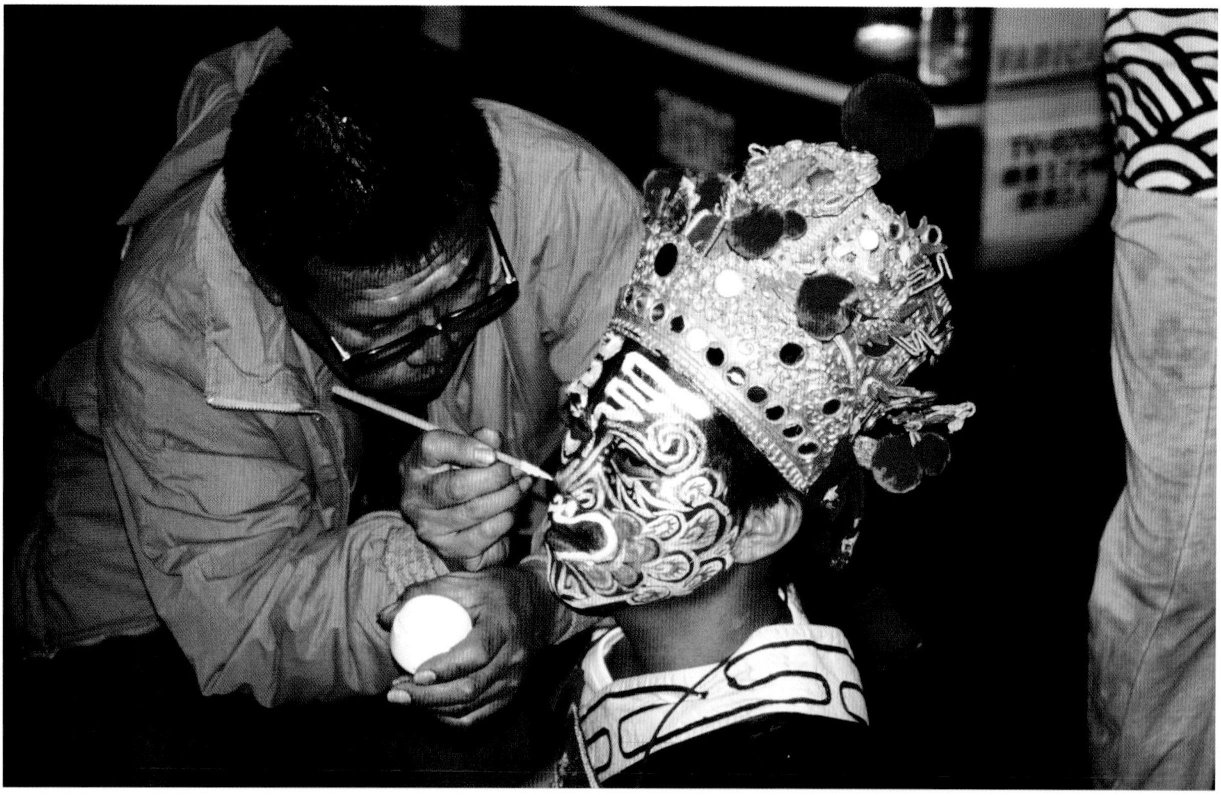

impressive to watch. For example, characters that move their arms around a lot might wear long, flowing sleeves. Other dances are performed with ribbons or weapons. Many performers learn the art of opera at the National Fu-Hsing Dramatic Arts Academy, which merged with another school in 1999 to form the National Taiwan Junior College of Performing Arts.

In 2001, the director Wu Hsing-kuo produced an adaptation of Shakespeare's *King Lear* in the style of modern Chinese opera. Experiments like this have increased opera's popularity and appeal.

One difference between Taiwanese opera and Chinese opera is that the music for Taiwanese opera is influenced by aboriginal songs. Instruments used in the Taiwanese orchestra include the *san-hsien* (SUHN-shee-en), which is like a banjo with three strings, and the *pipa* (pee-PA), which has four strings.

Taiwanese opera was created in the region of Ilan. Several troupes that perform the style are still based in Ilan and the region is home to the Taiwanese opera museum. Many famous female performers of Taiwanese opera only perform the roles of male characters. An example is the actress, Yang Li-Hua, who has performed male roles for over 30 years.

Above: **Chinese opera often involves a lot of movement. For example, an actor playing a warrior often performs impressive martial arts and acrobatics.**

The Penghu Islands

The Penghu Islands consist of sixty-four islands in the sea between Taiwan and China. The region is much drier than Taiwan and the islands are covered in grass and brush. These beautiful islands boast sandy beaches set against a lovely turquoise ocean. From May to October, their beaches are bathed in sunshine. The coastlines of the islands are dotted with small fishing villages.

The Penghu Islands are not crowded with people, although many tourists do visit them. Tourism is their main industry, followed by fishing. Some farming of peanuts, sweet potatoes, and sorghum also takes place on the islands, but it is difficult to grow

crops due to the windy climate. Walls made of coral have been built to protect the crops from the islands' strong winds.

The Penghus were along the route taken by explorers from Europe in the sixteenth century. In fact, a large fort dating from this time still stands on the Penghu Islands. The Portuguese were the first Europeans to visit the islands. They called the islands the *Pescadores* because of the abundance of fish around them. Later, the Dutch, the French, and the Japanese in turn occupied the islands.

Most of the people living in the Penghus are fishermen. As such, it is not surprising that most of the forty-seven temples in the Penghu Islands honor the goddess of the sea, Matsu.

Above: **The residents of the Penghu Islands are skilled in the use of a variety of boats. Here, small boats rest side by side on a beach.**

The largest of all of the Penghu islands is called Penghu. The island's only city, Makung, has a population of over 60,000. Lintou Beach, on the east side of the island, attracts tourists with its clean white sand. One side of the beach has an interesting military cemetery. Tourists also often visit Fengkuei Cave. Chinese tourists, in particular, often come to see the rock formations in this coastal cave.

The two next largest islands are Paisha and Hsiyu, both of which are attached to Penghu by bridges. Paisha, or White Sand Island, boasts a 300-year-old banyan tree. This enormous tree covers such a big area that its branches need to be held up by latticework. Walking under its branches is like walking through a tunnel or cave. The coast of Hsiyu, or West Island, has many hidden coves that feature beautiful scenery. The southern end of Hsiyu is home to the Hsitai Fort, which was built by the Chinese in 1883. On a clear day, visitors to the fort can see the mountains of Taiwan. Hsiyu and Paisha are themselves connected by the Cross Sea Bridge. This structure stretches for over 3 miles (5 km), making it the longest bridge in Taiwan.

Below: **Fishing is a major activity in the Penghu islands. Sometimes the caught fish are preserved by drying and salting.**

Hsiyu and a tiny, scenic island called Hsiaomen are also connected by a bridge. An arch has naturally been formed in the stone on the north side of Hsiaomen. The stone was gradually worn down into its arch shape by the waves of the ocean.

Puppetry

Above: **Although glove puppets are constructed to fit over the hand, they are made with detailed features and costumes.**

One of the most popular performing arts in Taiwan is puppetry. This art was brought to Taiwan in the early 1800s by Chinese immigrants. Over the years, puppet performances have evolved as they have been influenced by Taiwanese culture.

The main forms of puppet theater in Taiwan are marionette theater, shadow theater, and glove-puppet theater. Puppetry is an important part of Taiwanese culture and even plays a role in religious worship and folk festivals. The shows are not just for children, and the audiences are made up of people of all ages.

Glove Puppetry

Perhaps the most popular form of puppetry in Taiwan, glove puppetry has been greatly influenced by a Chinese form of musical drama called *pei-kuan* (PAY-kwuhn) theater. The story lines are very lively, and they are full of action and fighting.

Although the plots of the shows are often based on Chinese historical novels, the artistic style of the shows is distinctly Taiwanese. During fight scenes, for example, puppets perform martial arts movements in time with the music. Puppets can be seen fighting, jumping, and doing impressive somersaults. Taiwanese dialects are sometimes used in these performances.

Marionette Puppetry

Marionettes are puppets that are controlled by strings attached to their bodies. The puppets are about two feet (60 cm) high, and they are presented on a simple stage. These shows are performed as part of religious rituals to drive away evil or thank the gods. Marionette puppet shows are also held on occasions such as the eve of a man's wedding or a little boy's first birthday.

Shadow Puppetry

Shadow plays have always been popular in Taiwan. To keep up with the times, today's puppets and stages have become larger and more impressive. The leather puppets measure about twelve inches (30 cm) in height and are hidden behind a sheet which faces the audience. A light shines from behind the puppets to cast shadows on the sheet. The movement of shadows is what the audience sees.

Opposite: **Puppets dressed in colorful costumes make performances a feast for the eyes.**

Taijiquan

Many people in Taiwan practice taijiquan, which is also known as shadow boxing or *tai chi* (TY-chee). As a martial art, or combat self-defense sport, taijiquan involves learning series of postures that are performed in sequence. Taijiquan is generally performed alone, using extremely slow, focused movements, although it can be practiced in pairs, as if in combat.

The Taiwanese use taijiquan as a form of relaxation rather than as a way of learning to fight. The postures often require the person to imagine peaceful images, such as holding a bird in one's hand or embracing the sun. Taijiquan most frequently is practiced early in the morning, which many think of as the most peaceful time of the day. If you visit a park in Taiwan at sunrise you will usually see groups of people practicing taijiquan.

The movements of taijiquan are based around thirteen main postures. Performing the movements requires strength, focus, and sensitivity. The physical movement is a gentle form of exercise. Doing taijiquan helps people lower their stress levels

Left: There are many different movements in taijiquan. Some of them require the use of props such as the wooden sword held by this man.

and encourages a healthy flow of blood around the body, which has an energizing effect. During taijiquan, people focus on their breathing. This technique enhances flow of oxygen through the body, which is thought to enhance people's health and energy levels. Another benefit of taijiquan is that it can help a person improve his or her concentration. The focus required by the exercise helps people increase the amount of attention they can give to anything.

In any martial art, including taijiquan, a person must understand the opponent. If the person knows how the opponent is thinking, it is possible to predict his or her next move. This is one reason that the practice of taijiquan is done with slow movements. Moving slowly allows the person to understand exactly what each movement involves. Then, when an opponent is brought into the activity, the person is far better able to know where is his or her center of gravity, for example, and defend himself or herself.

Taijiquan has recently started to become popular in Western countries. The activity was imported to Western countries when large numbers of Asians immigrated.

***Above:* Many Taiwanese are very interested in taijiquan, and it is common to see groups of people exercising together in parks.**

Tainan

Tainan, Taiwan's ancient capital, is located on the country's southwestern coast. Although Tainan is the oldest city in Taiwan, with a population of about 750,000 people, it is only the country's fourth largest. The friendly people and warm climate throughout the year make it a lovely place to visit.

Tainan's past has given it a significant place in Taiwanese history. One reminder of the city's past are the ruins of Fort Zeelandia, which is also known by the names Imperial Castle, An-Ping Fort, and Taiwan City. The fort was constructed by the Dutch, who invaded the region in 1624, for use as a military base and trade center. During the Ming Dynasty, Cheng Cheng-kung and his son lived in the fort, which explains how it became known as the Imperial Castle.

Chih-Kan Tower is an important historic site in Tainan that tourists regularly visit. In 1653, the Dutch built this structure, calling it Providenita Fort. Later, Chinese immigrants started to

Below: **Unlike the other major cities in Taiwan, the streets of Tainan are still relatively quiet, with low volumes of traffic.**

call it "Chih-Kan Tower of Savages" and "The Tower of Red-haired Barbarians." Nowadays, stone horses and camels, as well as a row of nine stone turtle figures bearing stelae with Chinese and Manchu messages, can be seen in the garden of the tower.

In 1874, Shec Pao-chen, a Chinese officer, built a cannon fort in Tainan to strengthen Taiwan's naval defenses. This cannon fort, designed in a French style, took two years to build and is known both as An-Ping Big Cannon Fort and the Eternal Castle.

The Tainan Confucian Temple was one of four temples originally built by Koxinga's son Cheng Ching in Tainan in 1665. The temple has been expanded over the years, and it is now the most valued example of traditional architecture in the city.

Chi Tien Wu Temple is another historic landmark built by Cheng Ching in Tainan. The temple is dedicated to the worship of the God of War, Kuan Yu (kwuhn YOO). It is a grand structure filled with beautiful cultural artifacts. On one side of the temple, its roof is shaped in a curve. The temple also houses a central courtyard in which smoky, sweet smelling incense is burned.

Above: **The Tainan Confucian Temple was originally named the "Holy Temple of the Great Teacher," and a school teaching Confucian ethics was set up on its grounds.**

Taiwanese Temples

There are many temples in Taiwan. Besides being places of worship, these temples are also important centers of social activity.

The first temples were erected in honor of Matsu, goddess of the sea, by immigrants who came to Taiwan from mainland China. The immigrants suffered from various illnesses in their new home because of a shortage of doctors and medicine. Temples were thus erected to honor gods who were thought to heal illness.

The temples in Taiwan are decorated with some of the finest art in the country. These decorations include wood and stone carvings, sculptures, wall paintings, embroidery, calligraphy, and pottery.

Lungshan Temple

Taipei's oldest temple is in the Wanhua district. Legend has it that a man left a charm depicting the Goddess of Mercy, Kuan Yin (KWUHN yihn), on a tree. The charm started to glow brightly and grant people's wishes. In 1738, the Lungshan Temple was built in honor of the Goddess of Mercy at the site of that tree.

Below: **Devotees at the Lungshan Temple. Although the temple was built as a place to worship the Goddess of Mercy, it is often referred to as the "meeting place of the gods," as over 100 gods are worshiped in it.**

Above: **The complex of the Fokuangshan Temple is located northeast of the city of Kaohsiung. It is the center of Buddhism in southern Taiwan.**

Tsushih Temple

In the thirteenth century, Chen Chao-Ying tried to prevent the Mongolians from invading China. After his death, Chen was given the name Tsu-Shih, meaning "great ancestor." Chinese immigrants in Taiwan built this temple to honor Tsu-shih in 1769.

Tsushih Temple, located southwest of Taipei, is considered to be one of Taiwan's best decorated temples. The ceilings feature wood carvings depicting dragons. The walls and columns are also covered with carvings and Chinese inscriptions.

The Tsushih Temple has been rebuilt several times, after having been destroyed by earthquakes and wars. The third renovation of the temple has been going on since World War II—now, over fifty years.

Fokuangshan (Light of Buddha Mountain)

Founded in 1967, Fokuangshan, meaning Light of Buddha Mountain, is situated northeast of Kaohsiung. A complex of temples, halls, and gardens fills this mountainous area, and the giant statues of Buddha in the complex can be seen from a distance. During the Lantern Festival, Fokuangshan is a popular place for worshipers to visit. At this time, thousands of visitors travel to Fokuangshan to see the brillant display of lanterns.

Tea Drinking

For over a thousand years, tea drinking has been an important part of Chinese culture. It was the Chinese who first discovered the tea leaf and started this important tradition. A cup of tea in China holds more significance than it does in North America. The Chinese believe that the seven necessities of life are fuel, rice, oil, salt, soy sauce, vinegar, and tea. Tea drinking has been turned into a hobby and an art by the Chinese. Chinese immigrants brought this custom to Taiwan.

In Taiwan, old men often meet up for a cup of tea. Groups of two or three men will sit together around a small teapot drinking tea out of tiny cups as they chat.

To escape the hustle and bustle of Taipei, many city dwellers visit tea houses in the mountains surrounding the city. These tea houses are beautifully decorated with classical designs, and visitors can appreciate the tea and have a meal in the open air.

Regions throughout Taiwan organize tea-tasting competitions. Tea farmers, sellers, and experts enter these contests. When a

Above: **A tea-picker dressed for work carries a basket used to hold picked tea-leaves.**

Below: **Workers at a tea plantation take a well-deserved break.**

Left: **The Taiwanese regard tea drinking as an art, and they use special utensils, cups, and pots in their tea rituals.**

particular tea is declared to be good by the judges of a competition, it becomes popular and its price increases. In Taipei's tea shops, the shop assistants are knowledgeable about both the properties of each kind of tea and the 400-year-old tea steeping method that is used in most Taiwanese homes.

Tea is grown in Taiwan. The tea leaves grow on trees and are picked while they are still young and tender. Depending on the type of tea being produced, the leaves may be roasted or even partially fermented. The type of tea known as green tea is not fermented during processing and keeps the original color of the leaves. Black tea, called "red" tea by the Taiwanese and Chinese, is fermented before being roasted. In Taiwan, tea cups are usually white on the inside so the color of the tea can be seen properly.

The leaves are brewed in small, often decorative teapots. Small pots are preferred so that the strong aroma and the sweetness of the tea can be maximized. The purple clay ceramic teapots used during the Ming and Ching dynasties (1368–1911) are considered antiques and are extremely valuable.

In Taiwan, tea drinking is thought to be good for people's health. Tea's tannic acid is believed to have anti-inflammatory and germicidal properties. In addition, tea contains vitamins, essential oils, and fluoride. The beverage is also said to improve eyesight and alertness.

Typhoons

In Taiwan, the months from June to October are known as the typhoon season. Typhoons are tropical cyclones. About three or four times per season, a typhoon's strong winds and heavy rains blow across the country for up to several days at a time, often leaving trails of destruction. The environment is shaped by this regular occurrence, as soil is eroded by wind and rain. In fact, three-quarters of Taiwan's rainfall comes from typhoon rains.

One of the most famous typhoons to hit Taiwan in recent times was Typhoon Toraji, which came at the end of July 2001. Its winds reached speeds of up to 90 miles (145 km) per hour. Hundreds of homes were destroyed, and two hundred people were killed. Roads and airports could not be used due to the flooding. Power blackouts affected nearly 350,000 homes. Taiwan's crops and livestock were also severely damaged. In Nantou County, in central Taiwan, rice fields and banana groves were flooded. Mountain roads were blocked by landslides, and bridges were washed away. After the storm

Left: **Typhoons often cause landslides, such as this one, which blocked the main coastal highway in Taiwan.**

Above: **There is much disruption after a typhoon has struck. Roads are often closed to traffic as a result of uprooted trees and landslides.**

passed, rescue workers and over three thousand Taiwanese soldiers searched through collapsed houses for people who were injured or killed.

Although typhoons as strong as Toraji are rare, powerful storms are common in Taiwan. Just nine months earlier, Typhoon Xangsane swept across Taiwan, killing at least sixty-one people. Other smaller typhoons occurred between these two large-scale disasters.

Typhoons are always given names. In the past, their names tended to be Western names, as they were given by the United States Army. Since 2000, typhoons have been given local names to highlight the seriousness of the storms to the people of Taiwan.

Typhoons usually land in the southeastern part of Taiwan and move over the island in a northwesterly direction. Due to the formation of the land, typhoons in Taiwan follow seven basic routes. Typhoons crossing northern or southern Taiwan, as well as those moving toward the west or northwest, usually cause the most serious damage.

TPS

RELATIONS WITH NORTH AMERICA

Although the United States and Canada do not have official diplomatic ties with Taiwan, trade between these two nations and Taiwan today is thriving. In addition, many Taiwanese have emigrated to North America, and these people contribute greatly to the economies of the United States and Canada.

The United States has played an important role in helping Taiwan's economy to grow and become successful. It has also offered to defend Taiwan from any attacks by other countries. Despite these strong ties, however, the United States and Canada only officially recognize the government of mainland China, and they do not regard Taiwan as an independent country with its own constitution and government.

Below: **The city of Taipei is up-to-date with current trends. It is common to see brands such as Coca-Cola and Stila that are popular in the United States and Canada.**

On November 11, 2001, Taiwan was admitted to the World Trade Organization (WTO) as a special customs territory. Less than two months later, on January 1, 2002, Taiwan formally became a member of the WTO. Some Taiwanese believe that membership in the WTO brings the country one step closer to becoming a member of the United Nations. Taiwan hopes eventually to be officially recognized by all other nations, including the United States and Canada, as a country in its own right.

Opposite: **Baseball is popular in both Taiwan and the United States. The two nations played against each other at the 1995 Little League World Series held in Pennsylvania. Chen Ming-chen of Taiwan pitches during a game.**

History of Relations

After communists overthrew the Kuomintang in mainland China in 1949, Chiang Kai-shek's government moved to Taiwan. Although the Kuomintang now controlled only Taiwan, it retained the name "Republic of China" and it continued to be recognized on the international scene by the anti-communist Allies. The communist People's Republic of China on the mainland was not recognized. This meant that the government of Taiwan was allowed to represent the whole of China in the United Nations.

Military and Economic Aid

During the 1950s, the United States supported Taiwan with economic and military aid. The first help the U.S. gave Taiwan was economic aid after World War II. The U.S. gave money to the Taiwanese government to help build up the country's economy. When the U.S. stopped providing this aid in 1964, this forced Taiwan to fend for itself. The initial support from the U.S. was a great help to the success of Taiwan, and its economy started to thrive independently.

The U.S. also gave military protection to Taiwan on several occasions. In 1950, for example, President Harry Truman protected Taiwan against attack from China by sending American ships to guard the seas between the two countries.

Below: **American soldiers have helped to train their Taiwanese counterparts. The U.S. Marine Corps introduced Taiwan's soldiers to the training exercise known as "tossing the log."**

Switching Alliances

In the 1960s and 1970s, however, the relationship between North America and mainland China grew stronger. U.S. National Security Adviser Henry Kissinger visited China in 1971 and announced that U.S. President Richard Nixon would be visiting the following year. This visit signalled the start of U.S. support for China. By 1971, the U.S. supported China in its bid to become a member of the United Nations. In 1979, Taiwan received another blow when the United States established diplomatic relations with China, ended its diplomatic relationship with Taiwan, and closed its embassy in Taiwan. The Canadian embassy in Taiwan was also closed around the same time.

Above: **U.S. Secretary of State Henry Kissinger met with Chinese Premier Mao Tse Tung in 1973. This was one of many visits by U.S. politicians that led to the strengthening of Sino-American ties and the U.S. decision to establish diplomatic relations with mainland China instead of Taiwan.**

Protection from Harm

Although the U.S. and Canada sided with China against Taiwan in some ways, they have also offered great support to Taiwan. In 1979, the United States Congress passed the Taiwan Relations Act, which guaranteed that the U.S. would always protect Taiwan against any attack by China. This act was called into use in 1996. On the eve of Taiwan's first democratic election, Chinese ships performed missile tests near the coast of Taiwan. It seemed that China hoped to intimidate Taiwan at this important stage in its political history. Under President Bill Clinton's advice, the U.S. sent a large convoy of military ships to patrol the area.

Left: **Despite the lack of official relations, the U.S. government still maintains cordial ties with Taiwan. Here, U.S. President Bill Clinton *(right)* speaks with Taiwan Council Member Koo Chen-fu *(center)* during a group photo session for the leaders attending the Fifth Asia Pacific Economic Cooperation Ministerial Meeting, held in Vancouver in 1997. On the left is Chuan Leepak, prime minister of Thailand.**

The U.S. Stand on Taiwan

U.S. President George W. Bush continued to balance relations among the United States, Taiwan, and China. He supports a "One China" policy, discourages a Taiwanese declaration of independence from China, pledges military support to Taiwan in the event of a mainland China attack, and said that the U.S. would continue selling defensive weapons to Taiwan.

Special Relations with the United States

The United States plays a special role in Taiwan's foreign policy. Over one hundred agreements—covering education, customs duties, postal administration, air transport, and technological cooperation—have been signed between the two parties.

While there is no U.S. embassy in Taiwan, the American Institute in Taiwan (AIT), a private organization based in Taipei, facilitates business and cultural ties between the two countries. The AIT was established shortly after the U.S. government cut its diplomatic ties with Taiwan in favor of mainland China on January 1, 1979. The U.S. Department of State, through a contract with the AIT, provides a large part of the organization's funding and guidance. The U.S. Congress, in passing the Taiwan Relations Act, also assumed a role in overseeing the AIT's operations.

AIT's office in Taipei has a staff of over 300 and undertakes a wide range of activities representing U.S. commercial services, economic and political reporting, travel services, agricultural sales, cultural exchange, and military sales. It also operates a Chinese language school, a trade center, and a library. The AIT has a branch office in Kaohsiung that handles local commercial promotion, travel services, information and cultural work, and political and economic reporting.

Many of the world's other nations also do not recognize Taiwan as a separate country in order to protect their relationships with China. Taiwan, however, does have extensive economic and cultural ties with countries that do not have official diplomatic relations with it. Taiwan has established ninety-five representative offices in sixty-two countries and areas, while twenty-two countries have embassies and forty-six countries have representative offices, associations, or visa-issuing centers in Taiwan. Some of these designated trade offices perform the same diplomatic functions of the embassies or consulates.

Below: **Taiwanese President Chen Shui-bian *(right)* toasts Richard Bush, former chairman of the American Institute in Taiwan, in October 2002. Bush was awarded the Order of Brilliant Star with Grand Cordon in recognition of his contribution to U.S.-Taiwan ties.**

Left: **Taiwanese President Lee Teng-hui greets American futurist John Naisbitt** ***(center)*** **and his daughter Nana at the presidential office in Taipei. With the huge volume of trade between the United States and Taiwan, it is not surprising that business authors such as Naisbitt have a keen interest in the country.**

Trade with North America

The United States has long been Taiwan's most important trading partner. The country sells manufactured goods, including electronics, computer parts, and semiconductors, to the U.S. For the past decade, Taiwan has accumulated a large trade surplus with the United States, as it sells more to the U.S. than the U.S. buys from it. Since 2001, the Taiwanese government further opened its markets to U.S.-made products, and imports from the United States have increased. In 2002, the trade surplus with the United States fell to U.S. $13.8 billion. In the same year, the United States was Taiwan's largest trading partner, with two-way trade of U.S. $50.6 billion.

Taiwan ranks among Canada's top ten largest trading partners. The three largest exports from Canada to Taiwan are wood pulp, organic chemicals, and electrical machinery and parts. In return, Taiwan supplies Canada with computer systems and components, boilers and mechanical appliances, as well as electrical machinery and parts. Taiwan, however, exports far more of its products to Canada than the other way around. As with the

United States, these exports are mainly manufactured goods. Canada's Northern Telecom is also helping Taiwan meet its growing demand for cellular phone services by building many base stations to support Taiwan's digital communications system.

Taiwan has also learned from Canadian environmental know-how. Canadian companies are helping Taiwan reduce environmental problems caused by the dangerous burning of garbage and the polluting of the country's harbors.

Above: **General Colin Powell attends a book-signing at a Taipei bookshop in 1997. Powell, who became U.S. secretary of state in 2001, is one of several prominent Americans who have visited Taiwan in recent years.**

North Americans in Taiwan

There are many organizations in Taiwan that exist to promote a good relationship between North America and Taiwan. For example, the American Chamber of Commerce in Taiwan represents over 1,000 international companies. The chamber actively promotes the business of the United States, Canada, and other foreign countries in Taiwan.

Most North Americans who live in Taiwan are there to facilitate trade between the two countries. Several different states of the United States have trade offices in Taiwan. In the last few years, there has also been a trend of North Americans going to Taiwan to teach English.

Left: **Mina Sharpe is one of the many Americans living in Taiwan. Sharpe runs an animal shelter for stray dogs in downtown Taipei.**

Taiwanese in the United States

Taiwanese people began arriving in the United States in small numbers at the start of the 1900s. Large numbers of Taiwanese immigrants did not arrive until the 1950s. Most Taiwanese have come to the United States to attend universities. In 1950, there were 3,637 Taiwanese students in America. By 2000, the figure had increased to 29,234.

The number of Taiwanese immigrants to the United States has steadily increased. In 1980, there were 20,000 Americans who were born in Taiwan, but by 1990, the figure had gone up tenfold to 200,000.

Taiwanese American communities and organizations have been established throughout the United States. Taiwanese Americans mostly live in metropolitan areas such as Houston, Los Angeles, New York City, and the San Francisco Bay area in northern California. Among the organizations that serve Taiwanese people in the U.S. are the Taiwanese American Chamber of Commerce, the North American Taiwanese Medical Association, the Taiwanese Cultural Alliance, the Taiwan Engineers Association, and the Taiwanese Hakka Association.

Below: **Three generations of a Taiwanese family who have immigrated to New York pose for a group photo.**

A Hardworking People

Taiwanese Americans have had a substantial influence in the U.S. Besides studying and working hard, they also have a sense of community spirit. In 2001, members of the Taiwanese community contributed to relief work after the September 11 terrorist attacks.

The Taiwanese contribution to the North American business world has also been outstanding, with many success stories. Prominent Taiwanese Americans include David Wu, a United States Congressman; John Liu, the first Asian American to be part of the New York City Council; Dr. David Ho, who is renowned for his research on AIDS; and Lisa Ling, a reporter and a host on *The View*, a prime time television show in the United States.

Above: **Members of the Taiwan Merchants Association of New York gather at Hancock International Airport in Syracuse, New York, to show their support for Taiwanese president Lee Teng-hui.**

Taiwanese in Canada

Taiwanese immigration to Canada grew significantly in the 1990s, reaching a peak in 1997 with 13,321 immigrants. By 1998, the number of Taiwanese immigrants to Canada had dropped by nearly half, to 7,164 people. This figure has continued to drop, and by 2001, it had fallen to just 3,111.

Although over a third of Taiwanese immigrants to Canada from 1991 to 2000 were students, not all students prefer to remain in Canada, and many return home after their studies. In 2001, 6,000 Taiwanese students came to study in Canada.

Most Taiwanese immigrants to Canada, however, work in the fields of engineering, mathematics, and science. Others come with the intention of investing money or setting up businesses.

Almost all Taiwanese immigrants to Canada live in cities. The majority of Taiwanese Canadians are found in Toronto, Montreal, and Vancouver, often in close-knit communities. Taiwanese communities in Toronto are found in North York, Scarborough, and Mississauga. In Vancouver, the Taiwanese are concentrated in Richmond and Burnaby. In Montreal, they live in Dorval and Brassier. These areas have good schools, houses, and security, reflecting the fact that most Taiwanese immigrants are reasonably wealthy.

As in the U.S., there are organizations in Canada that serve Taiwanese immigrants and also contribute to Canadian life in general. These include the Taiwanese Canadian Cultural Society, the Tzu Chi Foundation, and the Taiwanese Canadian Association.

North American Tourism in Taiwan

Taiwan is an exciting destination for tourists, as it offers a fascinating culture, breathtaking scenery, artistic masterpieces, a full range of Chinese cuisine, and friendly people. Combined with this are convenient transportation, excellent hotels, and clean restaurants that permit travelers to explore the island's many attractions in comfort. Not surprisingly, visitors from the United States have been attracted to Taiwan. In 2000, they made up the third-largest source of visitors, with 359,533 people — 13.7 percent of visitors to Taiwan that year — coming from the U.S.

Cultural Influence

There has been some U.S. influence on Taiwanese culture, mainly through the expansion around the world of large U.S.-owned companies such as Coca-Cola and McDonald's. Baseball, Hollywood movies, and American music are also popular in Taiwan.

Below: **Visitors to Taiwan are often attracted by the country's unique buildings, which are designed in Chinese architectural styles. One such building that receives many visitors is the Chiang Kai-shek Memorial Hall in Taipei.**

Left: **On January 19, 1998, American movie star Kevin Costner made an appearance at the opening of the Warner Village, a cinema complex and shopping mall, in Taipei. Standing beside Costner is Taiwanese singer Coco Lee.**

The cultural influence of Canada in Taiwan is also becoming more apparent. Clothes designed by Canadian designer Simon Chang can be seen in Far Eastern Department Stores. There are five Roots outlets in Taiwan. Makeup by MAC Cosmetics, made in Toronto, is becoming popular in Taiwan, as is the music of Canadian artists such as Alanis Morisette.

Because of the large number of Taiwanese living in North America, the influence of Taiwanese culture has been growing. Taiwanese immigrants to North America have brought with them traditional festivals such as the celebration of the Lunar New Year. Taiwanese and Chinese food have also become extremely popular in Canada and the U.S.

The Taiwanese people have a very strong work ethic and this hard work has helped them establish vibrant communities that are an integral part of society in both Canada and the United States. Not surprisingly, Taiwanese immigrants to North America are often well respected by the local population.

Below: **Supermodel Cindy Crawford shared a laugh with Taipei mayor Ma Ying-jeou when she visited the city in March 2000 as part of a promotional event.**

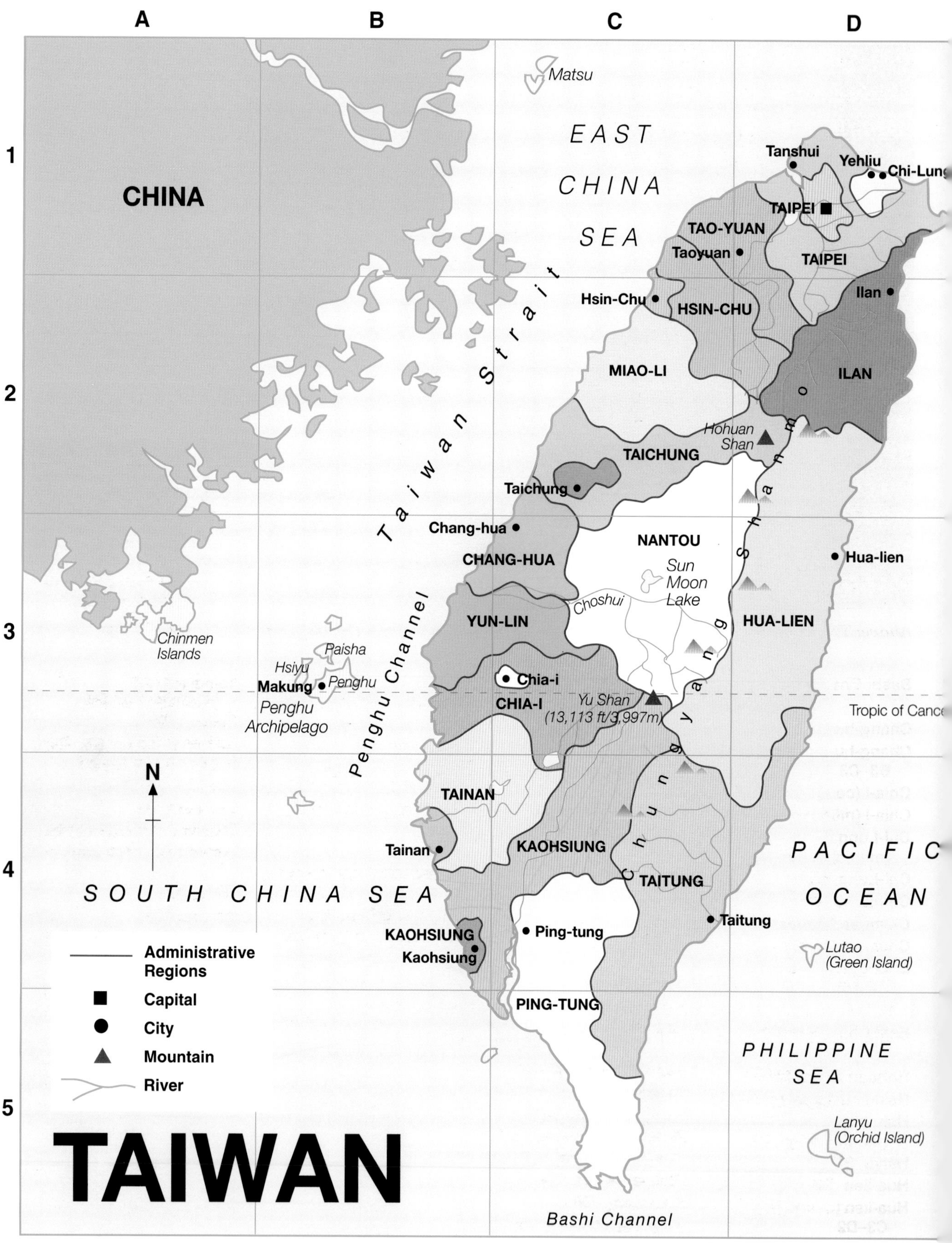

A
B
C
D
1
2
3
4
5
CHINA
Matsu
EAST
CHINA
SEA
Taiwan Strait
Tanshui
Yehliu
Chi-Lung
TAIPEI
TAO-YUAN
Taoyuan
TAIPEI
Hsin-Chu
HSIN-CHU
Ilan
MIAO-LI
ILAN
Hohuan
Shan
TAICHUNG
Taichung
Chang-hua
NANTOU
Hua-lien
CHANG-HUA
Sun
Moon
Lake
Choshui
YUN-LIN
HUA-LIEN
Chinmen
Islands
Paisha
Hsiyu
Makung
Penghu
Penghu
Archipelago
Penghu Channel
Chia-i
CHIA-I
Yu Shan
(13,113 ft/3,997m)
Chungyang Shanmo
Tropic of Cance
N
TAINAN
Tainan
KAOHSIUNG
PACIFIC
OCEAN
SOUTH CHINA SEA
TAITUNG
Taitung
Ping-tung
KAOHSIUNG
Kaohsiung
Lutao
(Green Island)
Administrative
Regions
Capital
City
Mountain
River
PING-TUNG
PHILIPPINE
SEA
Lanyu
(Orchid Island)
TAIWAN
Bashi Channel

Above: The Wen-Wu Temple is located on the mountains beside Sun Moon Lake in central Taiwan

Bashi Channel C5

Chang-hua C3
Chang-hua (county) B3–C3
Chia-i (county) B3–C4
Chia-i (municipality) C3
Chi-Lung (municipality) D1
Chi-Lung D1
China A3–C1
Chinmen Islands A3
Choshui B3–C3
Chungyang Shanmo C4–D2

East China Sea C1

Hohuan Shan D2
Hsin-chu (county) C1–D2
Hsin-chu (municipality) C2
Hsiyu B3
Hua-lien D3
Hua-lien (county) C3–D2

Ilan D2
Ilan (county) D1–D2

Kaohsiung B4
Kaohsiung (county) B5–C3
Kaohsiung (special municipality) B4

Lanyu D5
Lutao D4

Makung B3
Matsu C1
Miao-li (county) C2

Nan-tou (county) C3

Pacific Ocean D3–D5
Paisha B3
Penghu (county) B3
Penghu Archipelago B3
Penghu Channel B3
Philippine Sea D5
Ping-tung C4
Ping-tung (county) C4–C5

South China Sea A4–B5
Sun Moon Lake C3

Taichung C2
Taichung (county) C3–D2
Taichung (municipality) C2
Tainan B4
Tainan (county) B4–C3
Tainan (municipality) B4
Taipei (capital) D1
Taipei (county) D1–D2
Taipei (special municipality) D1
Taitung C4
Taitung (county) C5–D3
Taiwan Strait B3–C1
Tanshui D1
Tao-yuan D1
Tao-yuan (county) C3-D2
Tropic of Cancer A3–D3

Yehliu D1
Yu Shan C3
Yun-lin (county) B3–C3

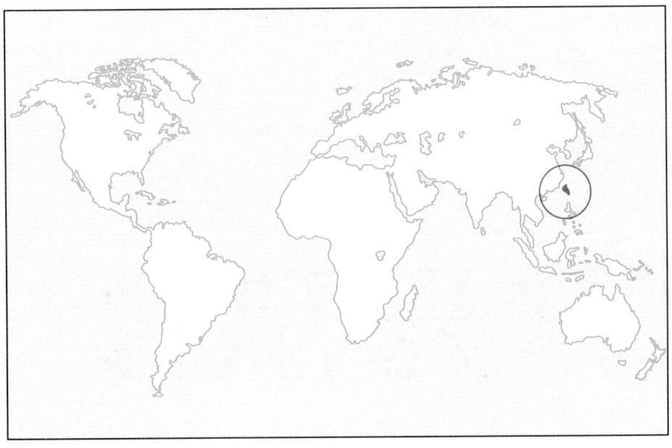

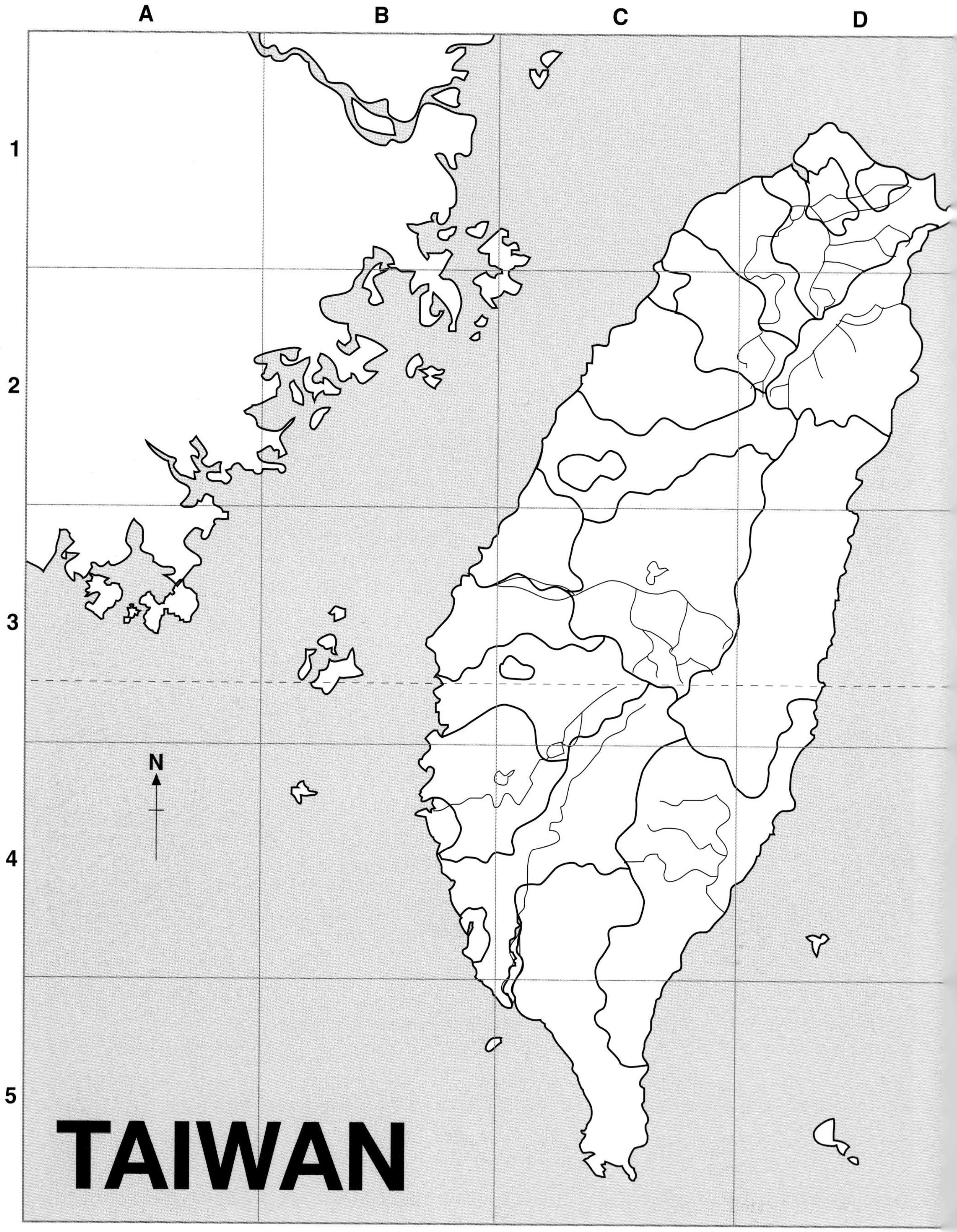
A
B
C
D
1
2
3
4
5
N
TAIWAN

How Is Your Geography?

Learning to identify the main geographical areas and points of a country can be challenging. Although it may seem difficult at first to memorize the locations and spellings of major cities or the names of mountain ranges, rivers, deserts, lakes, and other prominent physical features, the end result of this effort can be very rewarding. Places you previously did not know existed will suddenly come to life when referred to in world news, whether in newspapers, television reports, other books and reference sources, or on the Internet. This knowledge will make you feel a bit closer to the rest of the world, with its fascinating variety of cultures and physical geography.

This map can be duplicated for use in a classroom. (PLEASE DO NOT WRITE IN THIS BOOK!). Students can then fill in any requested information on their individual map copies. The student can also make a copy of the map and use it as a study tool to practice indentifying place names and geographical features on his or her own.

Above: **Yehliu, located along the northeast coast of Taiwan near the city of Chi-Lung, is known for its unique sandstone formations.**

Taiwan at a Glance

Official Name	Republic of China
Population	22,548,009 (2002)
Land Area	13,888 square miles (35,980 square km), including the Penghu Islands, Matsu, and Quemoy
Capital	Taipei
Highest Point	Yu Shan 13,113 feet (3,997 m)
Longest River	Choshui
Official Language	Mandarin Chinese
Major Religions	Buddhism, Taoism, Confucianism
Major Cities	Taipei, Kaohsiung, Taichung, Tainan
Administrative Regions	Sixteen counties (Chang-hua, Chia-i, Hsin-chu, Hua-lien, Ilan, Kaohsiung, Miao-li, Nantou, Penghu, Ping-tung, Taichung, Tainan, Taipei, Taitung, Tao-yuan, Yun-lin), five municipalities (Chia-i, Chi-lung, Hsin-chu, Taichung, Tainan), and two special municipalities (Kaohsiung, Taipei)
Famous Leaders	Chiang Kai-shek, Lee Teng-hui, Annette Hsiu-lien Lu, Chen Shui-bian
Festivals	Lunar New Year (usually in January or February) Birthday of Matsu (usually in March or April) Dragon Boat Festival (usually in May) Ghost Festival (usually in July or August) Mid-Autumn Festival (usually in August or September) Double Tenth National Day (October 10)
Currency	New Taiwan Dollar (TWD $34.66 = U.S. $1 as of 2003)

Opposite: **A guard stands at attention while on duty at the Martyrs' Shrine in Taipei.**

Glossary

Taiwanese Vocabulary

ben di ren (BUHN dee ren)**:** literally "people of this place;" the name adopted by Chinese immigrants arriving in Taiwan in the 1600s.

chi (CHEE)**:** energy believed by many Chinese to exist in humans, the Earth, and the universe.

Chungyang Shanmo (CHONG-yuhng SHUHN-mor)**:** the central range of mountains in Taiwan.

diabolo (di-a-BOH-loh)**:** a traditional Chinese toy, made of wood and shaped like a barbell, that is spun on a string.

hakkas (HAK-kars)**:** guests

hong pau (hon POW)**:** small red envelopes containing money given to children during the Lunar New Year festival.

Kuan Yin (KWUHN yihn)**:** the goddess of mercy.

Kuan Yu (kwuhn YOO)**:** the god of war.

Kuomintang (KHUO-min-dunk)**:** the ruling political party in China during the early twentieth century.

Matsu (MAH-tsoo)**:** the goddess of the sea.

pei-kuan (PAY-kwuhn)**:** a lively type of music originating in China.

pipa (pee-PA)**:** a banjo-like Chinese instrument with four strings.

san-hsien (SUHN-shee-en)**:** a banjo-like Chinese instrument with three strings.

taijiquan (TY-chee-choo-en)**:** a relaxing Chinese style of martial arts in which circular and stretching movements are performed very slowly; also called shadow boxing or *tai chi*.

tang yuan (TUHNG yuen)**:** rice dumplings that are eaten during the Lunar New Year festival.

yu (YOO)**:** the Chinese word for fish, which is a homonym of the Chinese word meaning abundance.

yuan (YUEN)**:** a branch of government in Taiwan.

English Vocabulary

aborigines: the original or earliest known people of an area or region.

amphibians: cold-blooded creatures such as frogs or salamanders that are able to live both on land and in water.

archipelago: a group of islands.

auspicious: lucky or bringing good fortune.

Buddhism: a religion started in India by Gautama Buddha that later spread to China and other parts of Asia.

couplets: pairs of pieces of paper on which rhyming phrases are written in Chinese script that are pasted on walls for luck.

demonstration: a public display to protest against an issue or a government.

designated: selected or assigned.

dragon boat: a long boat used in racing in which a team of rowers moves their oars in time to the beat of a drum.

enlightenment: for Buddhists, the final blessed state marked by absence of desire or suffering.

feng shui: an ancient Chinese set of beliefs and practices based on the idea that the placement of objects can affect a person's well-being and fortune.

fermenting: the process by which an organic substance is transformed by enzymes.

folk religion: nonmainstream religions that are usually passed down from one generation to another either orally or in written form.

foreign reserves: money that a government or an organization keeps in the currency of another country as a form of savings or investment.

headdress: a covering or decoration for the head.

impeachment: the act of charging a government service employee of improper behavior while in office.

inflation: an increase in the price of goods and services such that the same amount of money purchases fewer things than before.

judo: a Japanese martial art, developed from jujitsu, that uses quick movements and leverage to throw attackers.

karaoke: the activity of singing songs to the accompaniment of prerecorded backing music.

kendo: a Japanese form of fencing using bamboo foils or wooden swords.

loyalist: a person who remains loyal to a king or government.

marionette: a puppet that is moved from above by means of strings attached to its limbs.

martial law: law applied by military authority, usually when civilian government breaks down but sometimes by a dictator's government.

municipality: a primarily urban administrative division having powers of self-government.

patriotism: love, devotion, or support for a country.

percussion: relating to musical instruments that are struck to produce tones.

prefecture: a division of a country governed by a prefect.

reincarnation: a living being that contains the spirit of a being that is deceased.

reverence: a feeling of deep respect.

revolutionary: relating to a fundamental change in government.

sailboarding: a sport in which a person balances on a board as it is moved by the waves.

shuttlecock: the conical object that is struck back and forth in the game of badminton.

siege: the act of surrounding a well-guarded place in order to force the people inside to surrender.

silhouette: a dark image, as of a figure, projected onto a light background.

steeping: soaking an object in hot water that is below the boiling point; in tea-making, leaves are steeped to release their flavor into water.

stelae: commemorative stone figures.

stigma: a mark of shame or discredit.

tae kwon do: a Korean martial art, mainly for self-defense, that uses fast, hard blows with the hands, knees, or feet.

Taoism: a Chinese religion founded by Lao-tzu; believers in Taoism lead simple lives and let things happen according to nature.

unification: the act of joining together.

vascular: having channels for bodily fluids, as the sap of plants.

More Books to Read

The Abacus Contest: Stories from Taiwan and China. World Stories series. Priscilla Wu (Fulcrum)

Chinese Festivals Cookbook. Stuart Thompson, Angela Dennington, Zul Mukhida (Raintree/Steck Vaughn)

Taiwan. Cultures of the World series. Azra Moiz (Benchmark Books)

Taiwan. Enchantment of the World series. Alice Cromie (Children's Press)

Taiwan. Major World Nations series. Jessie Wee (Chelsea House)

Taiwan. Modern Nations of the World series. Robert Green (Lucent Books)

Taiwan in Pictures. Visual Geography series. Ling Yu (Lerner)

Taiwan: Nation State or Province? Nations of the Modern World: Asia. John Franklin Cooper (Westview Press)

Videos

Taiwan (Education 2000)

Taiwan (Questar)

Tug of War: The Story of Taiwan (WGBH)

Web Sites

www.ait.org.tw

deall.ohio-state.edu/bender.4/perform/pg2puppe/bdx.htm

www.gio.gov.tw

www.taiwandc.org

www.asianinfo.org/asianinfo/taiwan/about_taiwan.htm

Due to the dynamic nature of the Internet, some web sites stay current longer than others. To find additional web sites, use a reliable search engine with one or more of the following keywords to help you locate information about Taiwan. Keywords: *Cheng Cheng-Kung, Chiang Kai-shek, Ilha Formasa, Penghu Islands, Taipei, and Treaty of Shimonoseki.*

Index